DAIRY

KOSHER REVOLUTION

KOSHER REVOLUTION

New Techniques and Great Recipes for
Unlimited Kosher Cooking

BY GEILA HOCHERMAN AND ARTHUR BOEHM

PHOTOGRAPHY BY ANTONIS ACHILLEOUS

KYLE BOOKS

For my daughter Tess and mother Allie, in memory of my grandmother Goldie and
great-grandmother Tova, and for all the generations of women who have
communicated love through their food.   GH

For Richard Getke, still the best dining partner, even at separate tables. AB

Published in 2011 by Kyle Books
www.kylebooks.com

Distributed by National Book Network
4501 Forbes Blvd., Suite 200
Lanham, MD 20706
Phone: (800) 462-6420
Fax: (301) 429-5746
custserv@nbnbooks.com

ISBN: 978-1-906868-53-6

Project editor: Anja Schmidt
Photographer: Antonis Achilleous
Food styling: Susan Vajaranant and Geila Hocherman
Copy editor: Helen Chin
Production by Nic Jones, Sheila Smith and Lisa Pinnell

Library of Congress Control Number: 2011926467

Color reproduction by Scanhouse
Printed and bound in China

Contents

Foreword by Arthur Schwartz

Just as I was moving from my kitchen table to the computer to write this foreword, a wind came up and blew the loose galley pages of *Kosher Revolution* onto the floor. My kitchen now paved with recipes for My Miso-Glazed Black Cod; Ceviche with Avocado and Tortilla Chips; Chicken with Sausage, Fennel and Peas; Pistachio-Crusted Tuna with Wasabi Mayonnaise; and Cauliflower Paneer Masala, not to mention Bubbie's Brisket, I saw that this was truly a revolutionary book.

For a kosher cook, of the above list of dishes, which are typical of the whole book, only Bubbie's Brisket would have been both physically and psychically possible ten years ago. Where would I have found kosher miso for the cod? Who would have thought to marinate fish in lime juice and eat it "raw?" In fact, it was only last year that I found Italian-style kosher sausage. Kosher wasabi for the trendy mayo may not be brand new, but in kosher time, it's close to being so. Kosher paneer, a kind of cheese, a salute to our Indian and Pakistani neighbors? Well, you have to make that yourself—though it's easy following Geila Hocherman's instructions.

Jews have always eaten the food of the secular culture in which we live, adopting and adapting that cuisine to kosher dietary requirements, whether German, Polish, Russian, Hungarian, Romanian, French, Italian, Spanish, Middle Eastern of one kind or another, or what we used to think of as all-American. Nowadays, where I live, in Brooklyn, New York, pizza and sushi are by far the most popular kosher foods because they are by far the most popular secular foods.

Kosher is a set of rules, not a cuisine. Why shouldn't the kosher kitchen, encompass—nay, embrace—all the cuisines of the world, including the trendy chef-created food you see on television? Nowhere is it written that it shouldn't or can't. With Geila's "tool box" system, and with so many exotic ingredients getting kosher certification, there's no excuse for kosher cooks not to turn out interesting, even sophisticated, and, of course, very delicious meals every day and every holiday. *Kosher Revolution* shows you how.

chapter

1

Getting Started

Introduction

I'm a kosher cook with a mission to make kosher cooking indistinguishable from any other kind. Don't get me wrong. I love good traditional kosher cooking—comforting to be sure, but hardly "gourmet." I do it well, if I say so myself, and am always glad to add my versions of favorite recipes to the mix. You'll find some of them here. But my goal is to show you, whether you're a new cook or an old kitchen hand, how to make modern, blow-them-out-of-the-water kosher dishes—exciting, contemporary food—from wine-braised short ribs to chicken satay with peanut sauce.

To do this I offer an expanded culinary toolbox so you can make any dish you've seen and longed to try kosher, or convert dishes from say, dairy to pareve, with nothing lost in translation. Once you learn to recognize appropriate, best-tasting subs, you'll never have to settle for imitations of the "real thing," again.

There are plenty of other advantages to "kosher-revolution" cooking. There's the instant bump in the variety your cooking and menu choices will get, and with that the increased pleasure you'll give to all those you cook for. Your understanding of cooking anatomy, of the techniques that define dish making, will expand too, so you'll become a crack improviser, a creative kitchen force. And you'll gain flexibility—with your "kosher-revolution" pantry, you'll comfortably serve six in an hour knowing that you can, for example, add ground meat or feta, chickpeas and beans to stored Ratatouille Hash (see page 132) for a super chile—fondly known in my house as Chile Chilissimo.

Because I fell off the kosher wagon for a time, I know what trafe tastes like, and some of it is very, very good. So I can help you create the best, most diversely flavorful *kosher* cooking. While this book has only 95 recipes, it gives you access to every recipe there is. Once you see nonkosher recipes the way I do—as occasions for instant translation—you'll be able to cook kosher *anything*.

The Basics

We all know what makes kosher kosher. The dietary rules in a (kosher) nutshell are:

- Use kosher-certified ingredients only.
- All animals destined for the kosher table must be kosher-slaughtered and prepared.
- No shellfish, no pork.
- No dairy products served with meat.
- No fish and meat served on the same plate.

As in other areas of life, limitations can mean opportunities. It's all a matter of the way you think about what you want and how you go about getting it.

Your Menu Comes First

No dish stands alone. Each is part of a larger scheme—your menu. In cooking kosher, the choice of menu is particularly important, as meat and dairy dishes can't be served as part of the same meal. (Pareve dishes are, of course, a "free-pass.") Thus, what you make, and when it's made, will depend on your whole menu and when it's served.

Before I ignite a burner I always ask myself a few questions. Some of these may seem basic to you, but they bear mentioning:

- What meal am I cooking for—breakfast, lunch or dinner?
- Is the meal for "everyday" or for a special occasion, like a holiday? For the Shabbat or not?
- Will I be cooking for family or company?

Once you've answered these questions, ask yourself:

- What will I make? Will the dish be dairy, meat or pareve?
- What will I have to buy?
- What do I have on hand?

On the matter of bought versus stored items, it's important to strategize. I believe in the well-stocked freezer and pantry (see pages 17–19).

When constructing a menu keep in mind that not every dish can or should be a star; your meal must be orchestrated. I like a big-impression opening dish, a solid main, and a bang-up finish—a dessert to remember.

The important point is, for ease, versatility, and best eating, always think menu first and make a plan.

Read Your Recipe

The inspiration for the "kosher revolution" method began years ago, on the first day of classes I took at the Le Cordon Bleu Paris. The professor said, "Aujourd'hui nous faisons du porc à la bonne femme"– today we'll make pork braised with potatoes, onions and mushrooms. I had a moment of panic but then the light-bulb went on: I could substitute veal for the pork.

When, later, we embarked on the preparation of a chicken dish with a cream sauce, I had a similar epiphany: why not sub salmon for the chicken? This revelation led me to create my salmon with leeks braised in cream (page 69), a dish that's been the standout hit of many a dinner party.

The point is, when converting a recipe, you must first assess it. You'll want to know:

- which ingredients to change to ensure it's kosher;
- how to make certain the dish is *good* (assuming you'll have to substitute a "high-satisfaction" ingredient like butter for something else);
- when to regroup and create something entirely different.

Flavor and Ingredient Swapping

Finding the right ingredient exchanges is key to our revolutionary approach. You want to maintain the fundamental character of the dish you'll be translating while ensuring its suitability for kosher dining. Your new dish is bound to be different from the original, but that will be irrelevant once diners taste it.

For example, when I confront a shellfish recipe, I immediately think texture. What will replace shellfish mouthfeel? My first choice is a firm-textured oily fish, one that won't fall apart in cooking and that provides something of the shellfish toothiness. My answer is Chilean sea bass or salmon. The chunky fish works beautifully when steamed or stewed, and is a chewy pleasure to eat. I also find that shellfish pungency can be duplicated by the addition of a strong fish broth. For the delicious result of such a conversion approach, see Bourride with Aioli, page 70.

Some translations almost do themselves: For split-pea soup with chorizo, for example, all you'll need to do is sub kosher chorizo for the regular kind. Others require more manipulation—for example, lasagna. I challenged myself to make this a dairy dish. I read my recipe, which of course included ground meat in the sauce. In place of the meat I used sliced mushrooms (first sautéing them to rid them of excess moisture and then, because of their stronger flavor, decreasing their amount relative to that of the meat). I also lightened the dish, replacing some of the original cheese with a light béchamel. The result on page 126 is more healthful than the original dish and every bit as satisfying.

The Subbing Rules of Thumb

- Look at the bigger picture. You must aim for ingredient parity. If you substitute milk in a recipe you must also make up for lost fat and protein using, for example, a nut milk, which contains both. Exchanges must be delicious, but in addition to flavor, you must also consider food mouthfeel and temperature.

- Explore different cuisines, particularly those of Asian countries like China and India, which have a large vegetarian and low-dairy or no-dairy repertoire. Peruse vegan cookbooks, whose special ingredients not only taste great but are good for you. Seeing how other cuisines and dietary disciplines handle ingredients will help you sub effectively and add new flavor notes to your cooking. You'll also increase your range.

- Expand your fat repertoire. Think nut oils, like hazelnut, for example. Margarine and shortening have gotten a bad rap, but both work just like butter in cooking and baking—enabling pastry flakiness, for example—and add no flavor of their own. That's a great opportunity to add flavor—say, cardamom or lemon in butterless almond crescent cookies. Or pursue other options: my Macadamia Raspberry Tart (page 172), for example, has a crunchy nut-based crust.

- Translating recipes is, finally, about *learning*. The day I discovered I could make a fabulous buttercream using mostly Swiss meringue was a happy one. I even enjoy making mistakes so I can *learn* something. (I try, however, not to experiment for company.)

More About Texture

The basic dish elements are flavor and texture. Trying to translate texture when converting a dish can be problematic, especially when you need to thicken something—a soup, say—and your original recipe does so with "dairy."

Thickening often involves emulsification—the suspension of small droplets of one liquid in another. Emulsification is responsible for the texture of many sauces, such as hollandaise and vinaigrettes. Butter is also used with flour to make an emulsifying roux or, alone, as a final body-making addition.

To get around the "butter problem," ask yourself what will work like butter (or cream) to achieve an emulsion while contributing to, or not detracting from, best flavor. I've learned you can:

- Use oils by themselves to emulsify. Olive, basil or truffle oils help thicken while adding great flavor. Sometimes I combine olive oil with mashed roasted garlic that I've stored for a savory thickener.

- Use egg yolks in place of cream.

- Make a roux with oil such as canola or non-dairy fats. I've made terrific turkey gravy for Thanksgiving using the rendered fat from the turkey. Poultry fat also makes a great roux. (If you melt your own fresh chicken or duck fat, you get the bonus of gribenes—they're fabulous folded into mashed potatoes.)

- Thicken with ground mushrooms. You can use almost any kind—portobellos or porcini, if you can get them, are particularly good. If you want to make a dish that calls for meat and cheese, think mushrooms and cheese instead. You'll have something new, but better.

- Thicken with cooked puréed potatoes, onions, legumes and other vegetables.

Baking

There are three categories of kosher baking: dairy, pareve and Passover. Most of the world's sweet baked goods qualify as dairy. Pareve baking must be dairy-free and may require original-formula conversion. Passover baking must be flour-free, as no wheat flour may be used (except, of course, in matzo making). No yeast may be used for Passover baking, but baking powder, baking soda, potato starch and matzo cake meal are allowed—as, of course, are egg whites.

As with savory dishes, you're aiming for baked goods with the flavor and texture of their non-kosher counterparts.

For pareve baking, subbing oils, margarine and shortening for butter are key. The rules are:

- Which fat you sub depends on what you're making. For cookies that call for butter, as many do, I sub margarine. The resulting crumb is better than if you use shortening. (You'll need to compensate for the lack of butter flavor by adding flavorings like lemon juice or spices such as cinnamon or cardamom.)

- For pie crusts, I use shortening, or shortening mixed with margarine. Like butter, shortening and margarine remain semi-solid when cut into flour, making flakiness, which depends on layerings of solid fat and flour, possible. Nut crusts, which are of course wheat-free, are the crusts of choice for Passover baking.

- For cakes your options are butter, margarine or oil, depending on the crumb or cake-style you're after. Pound cakes, for example, require butter, so you won't be serving these in a meat meal. For other cakes, you'll use margarine or oil (or no fat at all), depending on the cake's moisture "profile," and/or the menu in which the cake will be served.

For pareve dessert making, I've also had wonderful results using nut milks in place of the animal kinds. Coconut milk and two relatively new kosher products—almond and hazelnut milk—are very useful in custards and pareve ice creams. Besides working like regular milk, they add special, subtle flavors of their own.

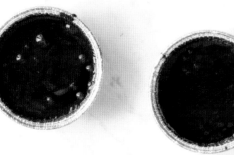

For Passover baking:

- Ground nuts—which contain protein and fat—can take the place of flour in cake making; they can also be used to make flourless pie crusts.

- Matzo cake meal, which is made from finely ground matzos, produces a finer-grained, tenderer product than regular matzo meal. Matzo cake flour is widely available.

- Potato starch can be used in place of flour, but you must use it with matzo cake meal. Together they make a tenderer, better-tasting product than if matzo cake meal, which has a "baked" flavor, were used alone. Ballpark proportions are: 8 ounces of flour equals 6 ounces of potato starch plus about 2 ounces of matzo cake meal. See individual recipes and The Chart for exact proportions.

- Use baking powder, baking soda and egg whites in the customary fashion for leavening.

Using this Book

At the head of each recipe you'll find one or more of the symbols M, D, P and PA. These stand for "Meat," "Dairy," "Pareve" or "Passover" and indicate the dish type and, where applicable, possible variations. The first symbol after the title denotes the "default" recipe version.

Convert It, which appears next to a recipe's method, is your guide to the ingredient exchanges that allow you to make, for example, a dairy or meat recipe pareve. Taken together, the Convert Its provide a distillation of "revolutionary" ingredient-exchange thinking. After reading a number of them, you should be able to make instant recipe conversions of your own.

The Chart, pages 198-201, is your go-to for exchange info at-a-glance. It notes food items by type and by ingredient options (indicating, for example, milk substitutions, such as almond or soy milk, for making pareve dishes). The brand names that appear in it represent the best products I've found for making the tastiest, best working exchanges. The Chart's Passover section is geared to baking and other dessert-making exchanges.

All of the ingredients are available online; see Sources, pages 202-203. Many can also be found in supermarkets, vegan stores, or Asian markets. When I first began cooking, the kosher pantry was almost bare. Now it's a cornucopia!

The Pantry

Non-Dairy Milks and Cream

Almond and Hazelnut. Made by blending nuts with water and then straining the result, these pareve milks are lower in fat and protein than their whole-fat cow's milk equivalent. They're also low-cholesterol or cholesterol-free. Use them as you would regular milks, but note that they taste of the nut from which they've been made—and are often naturally sweet or sweetened. I like to bake with them, as their flavors really shine in cakes and other sweets. In savory dishes they provide an additional flavor layer. I prefer Pacific Original nut milks, which have good flavor and mouthfeel.

Coconut Milk. Regular coconut milk is made by steeping grated coconut in warm water or milk and then straining out the juice. Lite coconut milk is prepared by diluting this liquid with water. It has about 60 percent less fat than the regular kind, and a less creamy consistency. I use Roland brand for both types.

Soy Milk. Produced in Asia for millennia, soy milk is made by grinding cooked soybeans with water. It's higher in protein than cow's milk, but lower in fat, and cholesterol-free. Most commercially available soy milks are clean tasting and add little flavor of their own. Look for non-sweetened varieties, like Kikkoman Organic Pearl.

Nut-Based Non-Dairy Cream. These nut-based products taste and work very much like cream. Unlike other non-dairy "creamers," however, they have no waxy mouthfeel. I prefer MimicCreme Almond and Cashew Cream, which is unsweetened and remarkably like the real thing. For whipping, I use almond- and cashew-based MimicCreme Healthy Top.

Oils and Fats

Margarine. This traditional vegetable-oil product works exactly like butter in baking and cooking, enabling, for example, flaky pie crusts and tender cakes. Because it has little flavor of its own, it invites the addition of dish-enhancing flavorings, like lemon or sweet spices. Kosher margarine is sold in a variety of forms. I use regular stick margarine only and recommend Earth Balance, Fleischmann's or Mothers.

Rendered Chicken Fat. Most kosher cooks are familiar with this time-honored ingredient, which can be made at home (render chicken fat over the lowest possible flame, stirring, cool and refrigerate) or store-bought, often from butchers. Similar to butter in its nutritional profile, it adds great flavor to many dishes, as well as providing body.

Rendered Duck Fat. A marvelous fat for frying or roasting potatoes, duck fat is more subtly flavored than chicken fat, and is high in beneficial unsaturated fats. It also has a relatively high smoke point. Save fat scraps from kosher ducks to render yourself or buy it online, see Sources.

Toasted Sesame Seed Oil. A staple of the Chinese pantry, this thick brownish oil, made from toasted sesame seeds, is for seasoning only. Don't confuse it with refined, almost flavorless sesame oils, which can be used for cooking. Brands I like are Mitoku and Eden Organic.

White Truffle Oil. Made from olive oil, or a mixture of olive and other oils, this versatile ingredient is infused with white truffle, or contains white truffle flavoring. I use it to impart richness and earthy flavor to a variety of savory dishes. It's especially good drizzled over finished dishes. D'Allasando is my brand of choice.

Stocks and Broths

Chicken Stock. To make chicken stock for the recipes in this book, prepare Be-All, End-All Chicken Soup (page 54) without the flanken. For "bought" chicken stock, I recommend Imagine Organic Kosher Chicken Broth, which is made with all-natural ingredients and has excellent flavor.

Imagine Organic No Chicken Broth. Vegetable-based and pareve, this works remarkably well as a chicken (or vegetable) stock substitute.

G. Washington's Golden and Seasoning Broth. This pareve vegetable-based powder is another good chicken stock substitute, and may also be used without dilution as a seasoning in, for example, dips.

Seasonings and Condiments

Miso. A traditional Japanese ingredient that appears most notably in the soup for which it's named, miso is a savory seasoning paste. It's made from rice, barley and/or soybeans. For the recipes in this book, I call for rice-based shiro miso, also known as white miso, or soybean-based hatcho miso. The brand I use for both is Mitoku.

Mirin. This traditional Japanese rice wine with sugar adds a touch of sweetness to many dishes. I use it in marinades, dressings, sauces and as a seasoning. My preferred brand is Mitoku.

Soy Sauce. Used in China for over three thousand years, this essential Asian seasoning is made from soybeans, flour and water. It should be naturally brewed rather than chemically produced—look for "naturally brewed" on labels. Pass by sauces that include hydrolyzed soy protein, corn syrup and caramel color, ingredients that denote synthetic sauce. Kikkoman is the brand I use most often.

Other Ingredients

Cheese. A vast array of "real-deal" kosher cheese is now available. Of the cheeses I call for, a kosher version of Parmigiano-Reggiano, Italy's preeminent Parmesan, is produced by Pietro Fanticini, a third-generation cheese maker located in Parmigiano-Reggiano territory. Gabriel Coulet, based in Roquefort-sur-Soulzon, produces authentic Roquefort with a heckscher. Kosher raclette, the semi-firm Gruyère-like cow's milk cheese, is available from Fromages Ermitage, cheeses makers in Vosges and Franche-Comté. There are many makers of kosher goat cheeses. Check the Sources (page 202) for these and others.

Chestnuts. This sweet edible nut is used in both savory and sweet dishes—and even as a snack. I call for whole, peeled and roasted chestnuts—peeling them yourself can be a chore—which come in foil bags. I use Galil, an Israeli brand.

Chicken Livers. If your butcher doesn't sell kashered chicken livers, which aren't otherwise available commercially, you must kasher them yourself following kosher law. To do so, remove any fat from the livers. Rinse them three times under running water and salt lightly with kosher salt. Transfer the livers to a rack that, when fitted in a roasting pan, will allow juices to run away from it into the pan. Broil the livers until well done, about 5 minutes per side. Cut open a liver to ensure that no pink remains, and broil longer, if necessary. Rinse the livers three times and dry thoroughly.

Chocolate. There are many brands of kosher chocolate available, both domestic and imported, sweetened and unsweetened. Before buying and cooking with them, read labels to determine whether the chocolate is dairy or pareve. Most dark chocolate is dairy-free. Dark chocolate brands I prefer include Swiss-made Alprose, Scharffen Berger and kosher-certified Callebaut, a wonderful chocolate that isn't, however, always available.

Extracts and Colorings. Kosher extracts, such as vanilla or almond, and food colors are widely available. I use Gefen, Bakers Choice and Bakto extracts for most flavors. Java Juice makes an excellent coffee extract. Look for Prima food colorings.

Konnyaku. Made from yam flour, konnyaku has been produced in Japan for centuries. It's extremely healthful, has almost no calories and comes in various seafood flavors including shrimp. I use it to make dumpling fillings. Don't confuse konnyaku (sometimes called konjac) noodles or jelly powder with the seafood-shaped product I call for, which is also sold as "vegan shrimp." The brand I use is shrimp-flavored Sophie's Kitchen.

Muscovy Duck Breast. A breed native to Mexico and South and Central America, Muscovy ducks have ample breasts with lean, deeply flavorful meat. By "breast" I refer to magrets, or two half-breasts. I prefer breasts supplied by Aaron's Gourmet Emporium.

Panko. Japanese breadcrumbs used to coat foods for frying or sautéing, oblong panko are flakier than their Western counterparts, and thus produce particularly delicate crusts. Kikkoman is my brand of choice.

Praline Paste. Used in baking and candy making, this smooth paste is made by combining equal quantities of skinned hazelnuts (or hazelnuts and almonds) and liquid caramel. When the caramel hardens, it's ground until creamy. I use Bakers Choice praline paste, which comes in tins.

Ramen Noodles. These fresh and dried Japanese noodles are made from flour, salt and water. It's the dried version I call for, available as Tradition Ramen Noodle Soup, a soup-mix kit that also contains a flavor packet. Use the noodles and save the packet for another use.

Sausage. A great variety of kosher sausage is made from virtually all meats—except, of course, pork. You can find merguez, andouille and bratwurst as well as sweet and hot Italian sausage. For the recipes in this book, I use sweet Italian sausage. Ask your butcher for his house brand; otherwise, Neshama makes many sausage styles.

Smoked Dark Meat Turkey. A fine ham substitute, this is widely available in two forms: legs (or "drumsticks") and "shwarma," which is made from the thigh. Either will do for the recipes in this book. The hammiest brand I've found is Aaron's Best. If you can't find smoked dark meat turkey, use turkey pastrami instead.

Surimi. A seafood stand-in, surimi is a traditional Japanese product. Kosher brands contain fish, various food starches, and seafood flavoring, among other ingredients. Sometimes formed to resemble the shellfish it's mimicking, surimi is best used in dishes like my crab cakes. Dyna-Sea is my brand of choice.

Tofu. A traditional Chinese and Japanese product, tofu is made from curdled soy milk. It's low in fat and cholesterol, protein-rich, and very nutritious. Tofu is available in extra-firm, firm, soft and silken styles. I call for firm tofu my recipes. I've used various brands of kosher tofu over the years, and all have been top-notch.

Wonton Wrappers. Made from flour, eggs and salt, these can be used in many ways not envisioned by their Chinese originators—to make kreplach, for example. They're available in a variety of forms, round and square, thick and thin. For the recipes in this book I use Nasoya square wrappers.

Zucchini Blossoms. These edible flowers come from the summer squash. They're available from late spring to early fall in specialty or farmers markets. Buy fresh-looking flowers with closed buds and store them in the fridge for no more than a day.

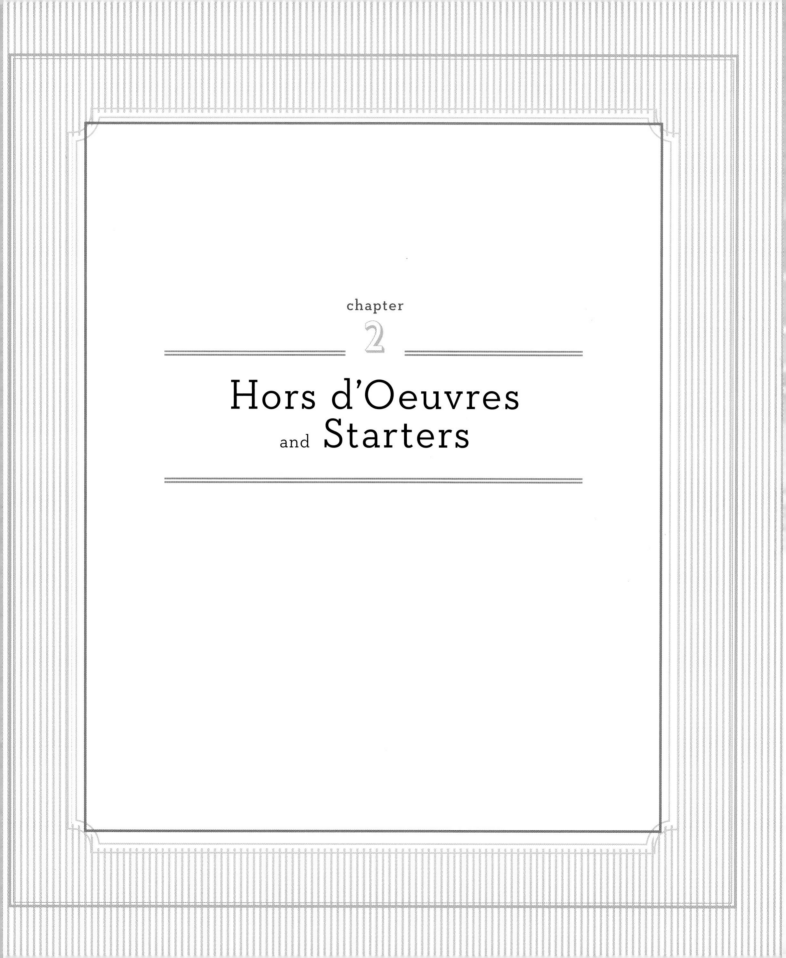

chapter

2

Hors d'Oeuvres
and Starters

Hors d'Oeuvres and Starters

"Revolutionary" starters begin with today's wonderfully expanded kosher pantry. Until kosher coconut milk became available, for example, you'd have had to pay serious kitchen dues to make the addictive—and versatile—peanut sauce accompaniment to Chicken and Beef Satays, a real crowd-pleaser. The availability of artisanal kosher cheeses has also made it possible to enjoy hors d'oeuvres like Roasted Portobellos with Goat Cheese and Asian Vinaigrette as well as any dish requiring real Parmesan.

Today's kosher pantry also boasts konnyaku and surimi, two traditional Japanese products that provide alluring seafood-like flavor and texture. I use the former in the filling of my Revolution Dumplings, toothy pareve bites that also rely on one of my kitchen staples, kosher wonton wrappers. With these on hand, you can make a wide variety of special hors d'ouevres, as well as kreplach, without any hassle.

Many cooks know that earthy shiitakes make a great meat stand-in, but think along with me, and you'll make meatless "meat" dishes that really excite. For example, I add pine nuts and tofu to the shiitake-based filling for Shiitake-Tofu Dumplings with Ginger-Scallion Dipping Sauce. The nuts give a "rounding" unctuousness to the filling whose flavor is mellowed by the tofu. There's no butter or milk involved, yet there *seems* to be.

I also like to "upgrade" fats to produce finer results. We all know about chicken fat as a dairy-fat alternative, but think beyond the box, as I did when creating Sautéed Chicken Livers with Warm Cognac Vinaigrette Over Wilted Greens, and use duck fat, which is free for the taking when you roast a duck, or available commercially. I partner my ceviche with avocado not only for flavor but to add non-dairy richness to the sprightly fish, which benefits from the buttery contrast while remaining pareve.

I'm particularly proud of the duck prosciutto in this chapter. Following an easy curing method, duck breast is transformed into "ham" that rivals the genuine article. I serve duck prosciutto with grilled figs, a traditional pairing, but it's truly a gift that keeps on giving. I use the uncut ends to make lardoons or julienne it to garnish soups or salads, and save the fat to use in pasta sauces. You get all the flavor of fine ham but without ham. Revolutionary thinking at its best.

Duck Prosciutto

serves 4

When people challenge me to "make trafe safe," they usually mention ham. This breakthrough recipe began with that dare—and my realization that what makes ham taste like itself has less to do with the meat than its cure. My quest for kosher prosciutto—nothing less!—led me first to smoked turkey leg, which is hammy all right, but hardly like the Italian specialty. I went to work, and, happily, scored a triple bull's-eye by giving duck breast a really easy salt cure—just fifteen minutes of prep followed by a "set-it-and-forget-it" refrigerator stay. The resulting "prosciutto" is so much like the real thing, but with a special character all its own, you'll be amazed. I pair this with grilled figs (page 26), a traditional prosciutto accompaniment, but that's just the beginning. Try it draped over melon, wrapped around asparagus spears or, diced and sautéed, as a salad garnish.

Geila's Tips

To achieve paper-thin slices, I use an inexpensive electric slicer, a great kitchen investment.

The very ends of the cured breast over-dry. Save them to put in soup. If you can't find muscovy breasts, place the meat sides of the two regular breasts together.

Two 6- or 8-ounce packages of muscovy duck breast (see page 19)

4 cups kosher salt

½ teaspoon ground coriander

½ teaspoon ground fennel

½ teaspoon freshly ground black pepper

1 cup white wine vinegar

1. Over a burner flame, singe away any remaining pinfeathers from the breasts. Rinse the breasts and dry with paper towels.

2. On a dish just large enough to hold the breasts, make a 1-inch bed of the salt. Place the breasts on the salt and cover with another inch of salt. Cover with plastic wrap and refrigerate for 24 to 48 hours.

3. In a small bowl, combine the coriander, fennel, and pepper. Holding the breasts over the sink, rinse with the vinegar (to remove the salt), and then under cold running water. Dry the breasts and rub all over with the spice mixture. Wrap the breasts, meat sides together, in cheesecloth and knot it at both ends. Using sturdy household tape (duct tape works well), attach one end of the cheesecloth to the top of the refrigerator interior, or hang the breasts from the inside of the refrigerator door, above and at the side of the top door shelf. Let the breasts cure until they feel firm but not dry, about 2 weeks. Start checking after a week. Thinner or smaller breasts will take less time.

4. Using an electric slicer or a sharp carving knife, slice the breasts paper thin or as thinly as possible. Serve.

Grilled Figs with Balsamic Gastrique

serves 4

(P)

There's nothing as delicious as fresh figs, unless it's grilled figs drizzled with sweet-sour balsamic gastrique. Quickly made yet impressive, these are perfect served with duck prosciutto, over greens dressed with a light vinaigrette, or with goat cheese. You can also use the Balsamic Gastrique as you would fine old balsamic vinegar, drizzled sparingly over savory dishes, or as the basis of a sweet-and-sour sauce.

Geila's Tip

Depending on the degree of ripeness, the figs may need to be cooked a minute more or less than indicated.

Balsamic Gastrique (makes ½ cup)

½ cup sugar

⅓ cup balsamic vinegar

4 tablespoons Balsamic Gastrique, made with light brown sugar

¼ teaspoon cracked black pepper

6 large ripe figs, halved lengthwise

2 tablespoons extra-virgin olive oil

1. First make the Balsamic Gastrique: In a small glass bowl, combine the sugar and vinegar. Microwave at full power for 30 seconds, or until the liquid has boiled and becomes syrupy. Alternatively, combine the ingredients in a small saucepan and bring to a simmer over medium heat. Reduce the heat and simmer until thickened, about 15 minutes. Let cool.

2. Transfer the Balsamic Gastrique to a medium bowl. Add the pepper and figs, and toss to coat. Marinate for 20 minutes.

3. Meanwhile, preheat an outdoor grill or broiler, or use a grill pan. If broiling, cover a cookie sheet with foil.

4. Brush the grill, grill pan or the cookie sheet with the oil. If using a grill or grill pan, grill the figs skin side up over medium-high heat until grill marks appear, about 2 minutes. Turn the figs and grill until just beginning to soften, about 1 minute more. If broiling, broil the figs skin side up until lightly browned, about 1 minute, turn, and cook for 2 minutes. Divide among plates, drizzle with the balsamic gastrique, and serve.

Liver Two Ways
Sautéed Chicken Livers with Warm Cognac Vinaigrette Over Wilted Greens

serves 4

I love chopped chicken liver, but sometimes I like to make a more elegant liver starter. This dish, which features the livers served over wilted frisée, combines the best of two worlds, savory appetizer and salad. The vinaigrette, with its shallot and cognac notes, is particularly enticing. I always follow this with a lighter main course.

1. If using the duck prosciutto, heat a small skillet over medium heat, and sauté the prosciutto until brown and the fat has rendered, about 4 minutes. Reserve 1 tablespoon of the fat. Remove the duck with a slotted spoon, drain on paper towels, and set aside.

2. Increase the heat to medium-high, or if using chicken fat, add 1 tablespoon to a small skillet over medium-high heat. When hot, add the shallots, and sauté until browned, about 3 minutes. Add the cognac, and reduce by half, about 2 minutes. Add the mustard, vinegar, sugar and olive oil. Remove the pan from the heat and blend well. Set aside.

3. Spread the flour on a large plate, add the livers, and dredge. In a large skillet heat the reserved duck fat, or the remaining tablespoon chicken fat, with the grapeseed oil over medium-high heat. Working in batches, if necessary, add the livers and sauté, turning once, until cooked through, about 4 minutes. Set the livers aside.

4. Wipe out the pan with paper towels. Return the pan to the burner, add the frisée and of the vinaigrette, and sauté, tossing, until the frisée has wilted, 35-40 seconds. Divide the frisée among 4 serving plates, top with the livers, sprinkle with the prosciutto, if using, and drizzle the remaining vinaigrette. Serve immediately.

2 ounces Duck Prosciutto (page 24; optional)

2 tablespoons duck fat (see Step 1), or chicken fat

2 shallots, minced

¼ cup cognac, sherry, or port

2 teaspoons mustard

2 tablespoons balsamic vinegar

2 tablespoons sugar

4 tablespoons extra-virgin olive oil

4 tablespoons flour

1 pound chicken livers (see pages 18-19 for kashering)

1 tablespoon grapeseed or canola oil

8 ounces frisée, rinsed, dried, torn into bite-size pieces

Chicken Liver Crostini

makes 12 hors d'oeuvres; serves 4 as a starter

People are sometimes surprised that other cultures have chopped chicken liver. The Italians do a great version that's spread on toasted bread—the crostini—and that usually includes capers. My take is temptingly herby and uses breadcrumbs, which give it a wonderful texture. The liver may be served while still warm, cooled, or even cold. Unlike the Cel-Ray accompaniment Bubbie's chopped liver got, this one demands a hearty red wine!

5 tablespoons duck or chicken fat

1 small onion, sliced thin and roughly chopped

1 sprig fresh rosemary

¼ teaspoon red pepper flakes

2 garlic cloves, flattened with the side of a knife

½ teaspoon fresh or dried oregano

½ teaspoon fresh or dried sage

2 tablespoons chopped small capers, rinsed and drained

½ pound chicken livers (see pages 18–19 for kashering)

½ teaspoon kosher salt, plus more

½ teaspoon freshly ground black pepper, plus more

½ cup white wine

2 slices white sandwich bread, crusts removed

1 baguette, diagonally sliced into 12 pieces

2 tablespoons extra-virgin olive oil

1. In a large skillet, heat 2 tablespoons of the fat over medium-high heat. Add the onion, rosemary, red pepper and garlic, and sauté, stirring, until the onion is translucent, about 5 minutes. Add the oregano, sage and capers, and sauté, stirring, until the onions are beginning to brown, about 5 minutes. Transfer the mixture to a plate and remove and dispose of the rosemary sprigs.

2. Add the remaining fat to the pan and heat over medium-high heat. Sprinkle the livers with the salt and pepper on both sides and sauté until cooked through, turning once, about 2 minutes. Return the onion mixture to the pan, add the wine, and cook for 2 minutes. Transfer the livers to a plate, and cook the wine until it has reduced to ¼ cup, 3 to 4 minutes.

3. Meanwhile, pulse the sandwich bread in a food processor to make rough crumbs. Add the livers and onion mixture and pulse until a rough paste is formed. Season with salt and pepper, and transfer to a medium bowl. Cover and chill, if not serving immediately.

4. Preheat the oven to 325ºF. Brush the baguette slices on both sides with the oil, transfer to a baking sheet and bake until lightly toasted, about 10 minutes. Spread the liver mixture on the slices and serve.

Chicken and Beef Satays with Peanut Dipping Sauce

makes 24 hors d'oeuvres; serves 6 as a starter

These satays are one of my favorite bites, but it's the peanut sauce that makes this dish so special. It's based on others I've enjoyed over the years, but couldn't make until kosher-certified coconut milk became available. You'll love the way its lime-brightened zing plays against the smoky meat, itself deeply flavored with garlic, cumin and ginger.

1. To make the satays, using a very sharp carving knife, cut the chicken and/or beef into ¼-inch-thick slices, 6 inches long by 2 inches wide.

2. In a medium bowl, combine the soy sauce, oil, shallots, lime zest, ginger, garlic, turmeric, cumin and cilantro. If using only chicken or beef, transfer the mixture to a gallon-size sealable plastic bag and add the chicken or beef. If using both chicken and beef, divide the marinade between two gallon-size bags and add the chicken to one and the beef to the other. Seal the bag(s) and marinate refrigerated for at least 1 hour or up to a day ahead.

3. Meanwhile, make the peanut sauce. In a large saucepan, combine the coconut milk, peanut butter and chicken stock and whisk to blend. Cook over medium heat until the mixture simmers, stirring often to prevent scorching, about 5 minutes. Add the tomato, turmeric, cumin, garlic, curry paste, if using, and sugar and mix well. Simmer until the flavors have blended, about 15 minutes. Season with salt. If the sauce is too thick, add up to cup water and blend. Cover and refrigerate the sauce for up to 2 days, or keep at room temperature if making the satays immediately. Just before serving, reheat and blend in the lime juice and cilantro.

4. Thread the strips accordion-style onto the skewers, one type of meat for each. Preheat an outdoor grill or the broiler or heat a grill pan or large heavy skillet over high heat. If using a skillet or grill pan, spray the interior with nonstick cooking spray or spray the outdoor grill rack; if broiling, line a baking sheet with foil and spray. Broil or grill, turning once, until the meat is just cooked through, 4 to 6 minutes total. Transfer the skewers to a warm platter and serve with the sauce.

Convert It

To make the peanut sauce pareve, substitute vegetable stock (page 195) for the chicken stock. Made this way, it's excellent served with grilled fish.

Satays

2 pounds boneless skinless chicken, light or dark meat, and/or sirloin, chilled in the freezer for 2 hours

¼ cup soy sauce

¼ cup canola oil

2 large shallots, minced

1 tablespoon lime zest

1 teaspoon grated ginger

2 garlic cloves, smashed with the side of a knife

1½ teaspoons turmeric

1 teaspoon cumin

3 tablespoons chopped cilantro

24 bamboo skewers, soaked in water for 1 hour

Peanut Sauce

One 10-ounce can coconut milk

½ cup smooth peanut butter

½ cup chicken stock

1 cup skinned and seeded tomato, cut into ¼-inch dice

1½ teaspoons turmeric

1 teaspoon cumin

1 tablespoon minced garlic

½ tablespoon harissa, Thai red curry paste or hot sauce (optional)

3 tablespoons light brown sugar

Kosher salt

2 tablespoons fresh lime juice

3 to 4 tablespoons chopped cilantro, to taste

Roasted Portobellos with Goat Cheese and Asian Vinaigrette

serves 6

Everyone loves the special earthiness of roasted mushrooms. My version pairs portobellos with goat cheese, now available in many kosher-certified types, and a sprightly salad. My secret is the Asian Vinaigrette, a real flavor powerhouse that's both hot and just sweet enough. This gets any meal off to an elegant start.

Convert It

To make this into a pareve dish, omit the cheese.

Geila's Tip

You can plate and refrigerate the greens and mushrooms and prepare the vinaigrette ahead. Bring the salad to room temperature and dress it just before serving.

6 garlic cloves

¼ cup extra-virgin olive oil

½ teaspoon kosher salt

3 large portobello mushrooms, stemmed, wiped with damp paper towels

Vinaigrette

¼ cup freshly squeezed lemon juice

⅛ cup soy sauce

2 garlic cloves, minced

½ teaspoon kosher salt

2 tablespoons sugar

3 drops hot chili oil

¾ cup grapeseed or canola oil

6 cups mesclun or other mixed greens

One five-ounce goat-cheese log, crumbled

1. Preheat the oven to 400ºF. Cover a baking sheet with foil.

2. In a small food processor, combine the garlic, olive oil and salt, and process until roughly puréed. Alternatively, mince the garlic and combine in a small bowl with the olive oil and salt, and whisk to blend.

3. Brush both sides of the mushroom caps with the mixture and transfer to the baking sheet. Bake the mushrooms until golden and most of their liquid has evaporated, turning once, about 35 minutes. Cool to room temperature and slice ½-inch thick. Set aside.

4. To make the vinaigrette, place all of the ingredients except the grapeseed oil in a blender and blend. With the motor still running, drizzle in the grapeseed oil until the mixture has thickened. Alternatively, place the ingredients in a large measuring cup and use a hand blender. Adjust the seasoning.

5. Place the greens in a large bowl, drizzle with ⅓ cup of the vinaigrette, and toss until the leaves are evenly coated. If the salad seems dry, add more vinaigrette and toss again.

6. Divide the greens among 6 serving plates. Surround one side with portobello slices and add crumbles of goat cheese on the other side. Serve.

Zucchini Blossoms with Two Fillings:
Sun-Dried Tomatoes, Basil and Cheese
Polenta-Corn Crème Fraîche

(D)

serves 6

At a picking farm one summer I was delighted to discover squash blossoms free for the taking. I've always loved them stuffed, and once home, set about devising my own fillings. Anything stuffed with cheese then fried is irresistible—thus my ricotta and parmesan filling, made lively with sun-dried tomatoes. The polenta stuffing is a corn double-whammy—it's got corn kernels as well as the polenta—plus crème fraîche for richness. Filled either way (or both), these make a terrific starter or hot hors d'oeuvre that's also fun to do.

Geila's Tips

See page 19 for information about finding zucchini blossoms.

The coating is a tempura-batter variation that produces a thin crunchy bite. Make sure to chill it, as directed.

¼ cup cornstarch

12 zucchini blossoms (see Tip), pistils removed, any attached zucchini retained (see Step 2)

Tomato, Basil and Cheese Filling

1 cup ricotta

1 large egg

¼ cup grated parmesan

¼ cup oil-packed sun-dried tomatoes, drained, cut into ¼-inch dice

1 small garlic clove, minced

1 tablespoon chopped fresh basil

Pinch nutmeg

Pinch kosher salt

Batter

⅓ cup all-purpose flour

⅔ cup rice flour

1 cup carbonated water

2 cups grapeseed or canola oil, for frying

Sea salt or kosher salt

1. Line a baking sheet with parchment paper and dust with the cornstarch.

2. Using a damp paper towel, very gently clean the blossoms, if necessary. (If a small zucchini is attached to a blossom, without removing it, slice it lengthwise into thirds.)

3. In a small bowl, combine the filling ingredients and blend. Handling the blossoms very gently, spoon or pipe 1½ to 2 tablespoons of the filling into them, twisting the blossoms to close them. Transfer the blossoms to the baking sheet and refrigerate until ready to fry.

4. Preheat the oven to 175°F. Fill a large bowl with ice water. In a second bowl that fits in the first, combine the flours for the batter. Whisk in the carbonated water just to blend; the batter doesn't have to be completely smooth. Place the second bowl in the first and refrigerate both until the batter is very cold, 15 to 30 minutes.

5. Heat the oil in a deep skillet over high heat until 375°F. Working in batches of two, dip the blossoms (and the zucchini, if attached) into the batter, shake off any excess and fry until golden and crisp, 2 to 3 minutes. Using a slotted spoon, transfer the blossoms to the baking sheet. Place the sheet in the oven with the door slightly ajar to keep them warm. Repeat with the remaining blossoms.

6. Transfer 2 blossoms to small warmed serving plates. Sprinkle with the salt and serve.

Polenta-Corn Crème Fraîche Filling

(D)

I use store-bought, prepared polenta for this, but you can make your own, if you like.

1. Bring a medium pot of water to a boil. Add the corn and cook just until tender, about 2 minutes. Drain, cool the corn, and cut off the kernels. Transfer to a medium bowl and set aside.

2. Heat the butter and oil in a medium sauté pan over medium heat. Add the onion and jalapeño and sauté, stirring, until the onion is translucent and the pepper soft, about 10 minutes. Transfer to the corn bowl, add the polenta and crème fraîche, and season with the salt and pepper. Blend well, stuff the blossoms with the filling, and fry as directed opposite.

2 ears of corn, or 1 cup frozen and defrosted corn kernels

1 tablespoon unsalted butter

1 tablespoon canola oil

1 small onion, chopped

1 jalapeño pepper, seeded, minced

1 cup prepared polenta, soft

½ cup crème fraîche

Kosher salt and freshly ground black pepper

Ceviche with Avocado and Tortilla Chips ⓟ

serves 6

Here's a confession: I never serve gefilte fish. That favorite has been replaced on my table by this more exciting dish, which will do wonders for your menu as a starter or light main. Tangy with fresh lime, the ceviche also pairs buttery avocado and crunchy chips, a terrific textural play. And most of the dish is made ahead, a big plus when you've got other cooking to do.

Geila's Tips

To dismantle an avocado for slicing, first cut it lengthwise and gently twist the halves apart. Embed the pit on the blade-heel of a large knife, twist, and lift to remove the pit. Peel the avocado, then slice the flesh as required.

I've found that jalapeños with a brown line or veins on the outside are hotter than those without.

1½ pounds fluke, flounder or other non-oily, white-fleshed fish, cut into bite-size pieces (about 1-inch square)

1 medium tomato, skinned, seeded and cut into ¼-inch dice

4 scallions, white parts only, sliced thin

½ cup chopped cilantro

½ cup of mango, cut into ¼-inch dice (optional)

2 garlic cloves, minced

½ jalapeño, seeded and minced

⅓ cup fruity, extra-virgin olive oil

⅓ cup freshly squeezed lime juice

½ teaspoon kosher salt, or to taste

2 avocados, sliced ¼ inch thick

Tortilla chips, for serving

1. In a medium nonreactive bowl, combine the fish, tomato, scallions, cilantro and mango, if using.

2. In a separate small bowl or large measuring cup, combine the garlic, jalapeño, oil, lime juice and salt, and stir to blend. Pour the mixture over the fish and toss gently. Cover and refrigerate for at least 3 hours.

3. Using a slotted spoon, fill a 4-ounce ramekin with the ceviche. Tip to drain any excess liquid and unmold onto the center of each serving plate. Alternatively, mound portions of the ceviche onto the plates. Fan the avocado around the ceviche, garnish with the chips, and serve.

Mango Salad with Sherry-Shallot Vinaigrette (P)

serves 6

I never tire of this salad. What makes it so special is its play of sweet and tart—of delectable mango with sherry vinegar and shallot bite. Arugula, endive and toasted pine nuts add more flavor layers. Mango is now available all year round. For this recipe, I always choose slightly under-ripe fruit, which is tarter than more mature kinds, but either will do. You can gild the lily by garnishing the salad with crumbled feta or blue cheese, but it's great as is.

Geila's Tip

You may not need all the dressing the recipe makes, but any extra is money in the fridge. Use it for salads made with peaches or other fruit, or tart or bitter greens, such as endives or chicory.

½ cup plus 1 teaspoon canola oil

½ cup pine nuts

2 large shallots, roughly chopped

¼ cup sherry vinegar

2 tablespoons fresh lemon juice

½ teaspoon kosher salt or more, if needed

2 tablespoons honey

¼ cup extra-virgin olive oil

6 cups baby arugula

2 medium heads endive, sliced into 1-inch pieces

½ cup red onion sliced thin

1 cup mango, cut into 1-inch dice

1. In a small frying pan, heat the 1 teaspoon of oil over medium-low heat. Add the pine nuts and toast them, tossing frequently, until lightly colored and fragrant, about 3 minutes. Set aside.

2. In a large measuring cup, combine the shallots, vinegar, lemon juice, salt, honey, olive oil and remaining canola oil. Using a hand or stand blender, blend well. Adjust the seasoning, if necessary.

3. In a large serving bowl, combine the arugula, endive, onions, mango, and the toasted pine nuts. Drizzle over half of the dressing and toss. Add more dressing if the salad seems dry. Adjust the seasoning, toss again, and serve.

Dumplings Two Ways
Revolution Dumplings with Orange-Ginger Dipping Sauce
makes 48

(P)

Sometimes fate hands you just what you're looking for. A while ago I was planning an Asian-themed cocktail party and dared myself to make pareve "shrimp"-filled dumplings. My challenge took me to Chinatown where I discovered (in a vegan grocery store!) konnyaku, a traditional Japanese product made from yam flour. It comes in various flavors including shrimp.

These delicious dumplings can be steamed, fried or simmered, and all three options are given below, but the last must be done watchfully as the wrappers can break if the water boils. No need to worry about elaborate wrapper pleating; the basic triangular kreplach fold works beautifully.

1. Using a food processor, pulse the konnyaku until it's finely chopped. Transfer to a medium bowl and combine with the remaining dumpling ingredients except the wonton skins. Stir to blend.

2. To form the dumplings, place about 1 teaspoon of the filling in the center of each wrapper. Moisten two edges of the wrapper with water, fold to make a triangle, and press the edges to seal in the filling.

3. Preheat the oven to 200ºF and put a pan of hot water in it, for moisture. To steam the dumplings, use either a bamboo steamer or a roasting pan with a fitted rack. In a pot, if using the steamer, or in the roasting pan, bring ¼ to ½ inch of water to a simmer over medium heat. Line the steamer with cabbage leaves and lightly spray with nonstick vegetable cooking spray, or spray the steamer's surface or rack lightly. Place as many dumplings as will fit into the steamer, or onto the rack, without touching each other. Cover and steam until the edges of the wrappers appear soft, 3 to 5 minutes. Transfer the dumplings from the steamer or rack to a heatproof platter and place in the oven to keep warm. Repeat until all the dumplings are cooked.

To fry the dumplings, heat a large nonstick skillet on medium-high heat. Add 1 tablespoon vegetable oil and when hot, add as many dumplings as will comfortable fit. Sauté, turning once, until lightly brown, about 1 minute per side. Repeat until all the dumplings are cooked. To simmer the dumplings, fill a roasting pan three-quarters full with water. Bring the water to a boil, reduce the heat to barely simmering, and slide in as many dumplings as will comfortably fit. Simmer until the wrapper edges appear soft, about 5 minutes. Remove with a perforated spoon and repeat until all the dumplings are cooked. Keep warm as directed above.

4. Meanwhile, to make the dipping sauce, combine the soy sauce, ginger and orange juice with 2 tablespoons of water.

5. Transfer the dumplings to serving plates and serve with the sauce.

Geila's Tips

Uncooked dumplings freeze very well. Place them on a baking sheet, sprinkle with cornstarch (to prevent sticking), freeze, then transfer to a plastic bag for freezer storage.

If you have difficulty finding konnyaku, you can use surimi, a fish-based product that has a distinct shrimp flavor.

Dumplings

One 6- or 8-ounce package of shrimp-style konnyaku, or shrimp surimi

⅓ cup diced water chestnuts

¼ cup thinly sliced scallion, white parts and a bit of green

¼ cup chopped cilantro

1 egg white

1 tablespoon soy sauce

1 tablespoon mirin

1 tablespoon toasted sesame oil

¼ teaspoon chili oil

One 48-piece package wonton wrappers

Dipping Sauce

¼ cup soy sauce

1½ teaspoons grated ginger

2 tablespoons orange juice

Shiitake-Tofu Dumplings with Ginger-Scallion Dipping Sauce

(P)

makes 48

I devised these delicious dumplings to pair with my konnyaku-based version, whose filling tastes like shrimp. I wanted something pareve that also tasted meaty. I thought of shiitake mushrooms, which have a meaty savor—too much so, it turned out. So I added tofu, which tamed the shiitakes perfectly. I also included napa cabbage for crunch. Served with a sprightly ginger-based dipping sauce, these make a perfect nibble.

Geila's Tip

These can also be fried; see Step 3, page 41.

3 ounces dried shiitake mushrooms

¾ cup pine nuts

4 ounces firm tofu, drained on a paper towel

3 cups Napa cabbage sliced fine (about 8 ounces), plus leaves, for lining a steamer

4 garlic cloves, roasted

2 tablespoons soy sauce

1 teaspoon grated or minced ginger

1 tablespoon mirin

2 tablespoons rice vinegar

Kosher salt

½ teaspoon hot chili oil (optional)

1 egg white, if needed

One 48-piece package wonton wrappers

Dipping Sauce

3 tablespoons soy sauce

1 scallion, white part only, minced

1 teaspoon gated ginger

3 drops hot chili oil

1 tablespoon sugar

1. Place the mushrooms in a small bowl and add hot water to cover. Soak until the mushrooms are soft, about 30 minutes.

2. Drain the mushrooms (strain and reserve the soaking liquid for soup or stock) and transfer to a food processor. Add the nuts, tofu, cabbage, and garlic. Pulse until chopped fine, and transfer to a medium bowl. Add the soy sauce, ginger, mirin, and vinegar. Season with the salt, add the chili oil, if using, and blend. If the mixture seems crumbly, add the egg white and mix well.

3. Place wonton wrappers on a work surface. Place 1 teaspoon of the filling in the center of the wrappers. Moisten two adjacent edges with water, fold to make a triangle. Seal the dumplings by pressing the edges. Repeat with the remaining wrappers.

4. Preheat the oven to 200ºF. and put a pan of hot water in it, for moisture. To steam the dumplings, use either a bamboo steamer or a roasting pan with a fitted rack. In a pot, if using the steamer, or in the roasting pan, bring ¼ to ½ inch of water to a simmer over medium heat. Line the steamer with cabbage leaves and lightly spray with nonstick vegetable cooking spray, or spray the steamer's surface or rack lightly with it. Place as many dumplings as will fit into the steamer, or on the rack, without touching each other. Cover and steam until the edges of the wrappers appear of, 3 to 5 minutes. Transfer the dumplings to a heatproof platter and place in the oven to keep warm. Repeat until all the dumplings are cooked.

5. Meanwhile, to make the dipping sauce, in a small bowl, combine all the ingredients plus 3 tablespoons water and stir.

6. Transfer the dumplings to plates and serve with the sauce.

Fried Pea and Parmesan Ravioli

makes 24 hors d'oeuvres; serves 6 as a starter

(D)

You probably don't think of peas and Parmesan as a culinary combo, but they're fabulous together. These quick-to-do fried ravioli feature a filling made from that coupling plus ricotta for creaminess and a bit of mint, a real pea flavor-enhancer. The wonton wrappers fry beautifully—my hors d'oeuvre pantry would be bare without them. These make a great starter, too.

1. Put the peas in a colander and place under hot running water to defrost them. Drain and set aside.

2. In a small frying pan, heat the 1 teaspoon of oil over medium-low heat. Add the pine nuts and toast them, tossing frequently, until lightly colored and fragrant, about 3 minutes. Transfer the nuts to a food processor.

3. Add the peas, ricotta, Parmesan, garlic, salt, nutmeg and mint to the processor and pulse until a paste is formed. Adjust the seasoning, if necessary.

4. Line a cookie sheet with parchment paper. Place 4 wrappers on a dry work surface. Place 1 tablespoon of the filling in the center of each, brush two adjacent edges with a little water (or use your fingertip), fold on the diagonal, and pinch to seal. Repeat with the remaining filling and wrappers. If not frying immediately, refrigerate or freeze the ravioli.

5. Fill a large heavy skillet with ½ inch of oil and heat over medium heat until the oil is 350°F. Alternatively, test the heat of the oil by placing a corner of a ravioli in it; the oil is ready if the corner sizzles. Working in batches, fry the ravioli without crowding until lightly golden (see Tip), turning once with a slotted spoon, about 2 minutes. Transfer the ravioli to paper towels and sprinkle with salt. Transfer to a serving dish and serve.

Geila's Tip

Remove the ravioli from the oil while they're one shade lighter than you want them to be. They'll continue to color after cooking.

8 ounces frozen peas

1 teaspoon grapeseed or canola oil, plus more for frying

¼ cup pine nuts

1 cup ricotta, drained using a colander or strainer

¼ cup grated Parmesan

1 garlic clove

½ teaspoon kosher salt, plus more for sprinkling

⅛ teaspoon nutmeg

2 tablespoons chopped mint

24 wonton wrappers

chapter

3

Soups

Soups

Soups are at the heart of kosher cooking—think golden chicken soup. Until now, though, many soups that use cream for richness or pork for heartiness, not to mention uncertified ingredients, were beyond the kosher cook's reach. With the "revolutionary" approach, however, the world of soups, earthy to elegant, can be made for kosher enjoyment— and their recipes converted for meat, dairy, and pareve dining.

Take Velvet Chestnut Soup, a lusciously elegant starter. With the advent of kosher-certified roasted chestnuts and truffle oil, this terrific "meat" dish is not only doable, but can be made dairy or pareve without compromise. Kosher coconut milk, another newcomer to the kosher pantry, enriches Coconut-Ginger Squash Soup, an Asian-themed pareve dish than can also be "meat." Lentil Soup with "Ham" gets its hearty, ham-like smokiness from smoked turkey drumstick and, using Parmesan rind, can be a dairy dish too. The rind also flavors Fresh Vegetable Minestrone, where it elevates a dish that, before kosher Parmesan was available, often lacked character.

But "revolutionary" soups aren't about "new" flavors only. A creamy soup that's also pareve needs to have the same mouthfeel as one made with dairy products or starches. Four-Mushroom Onion Soup with Truffle Oil-Thyme Croûtes uses oil to provide body as does the pareve variation of Roasted

Eggplant and Pepper Soup with Fricos. So many of the recipes in this chapter can be made for alternative menus that one recipe turns out to be two or three recipes.

Of course, I couldn't do this chapter without including that essential soup I mentioned at the start. Be-All, End-All Chicken Soup is just that—the best version of this soul-satisfying brew you'll ever enjoy. I honor the classic formula, but add flanken for flavor depth; I've also refined the method so you get a soup that's beautifully clear without having to clarify it. There's a kreplach recipe that, non-traditionally but super-conveniently, uses wonton wrappers. They're yet another example of a newly available kosher ingredient that, joined to innovative techniques, equals revolutionary soup making.

Roasted Eggplant and Pepper Soup with Fricos

serves 10 to 12

I love this delectable soup, which is full of the deep flavors of roasted eggplant and sweet peppers. It's also a great example of three-way cooking—a single dish you can easily modify to make something that works for any menu. The option to finish thickening the soup with oil rather than with butter or a butter-based roux is key to its versatility. I offer this with fricos—quickly prepared cheese wafers—but you could garnish it with grated Parmesan and fresh ricotta instead.

Convert It

To make this into a meat dish, substitute chicken stock for the vegetable stock and drizzle each serving with Balsamic Gastrique (page 26). For a pareve version, substitute extra-virgin olive oil for the butter, and finish with drops of balsamic vinegar, Balsamic Gastrique or basil leaves.

Geila's Tip

You can make the fricos ahead of time and store them in an airtight container. They're also delicious served with drinks.

4 medium to large eggplants (4 to 5 pounds)

6 medium red, yellow or orange bell peppers

2 tablespoons butter

3 tablespoons grapeseed or canola oil

2 large onions, coarsely chopped

4 to 6 large garlic cloves, to taste, minced

One 2-ounce can tomato paste

3 quarts vegetable stock

Salt and freshly ground black pepper

3 or 4 fresh basil leaves

Fricos

1 cup shredded Parmesan, Cheddar, Swiss or other hard cheese

1½ to 2 tablespoons all-purpose flour

¼ teaspoon cayenne pepper, or to taste

1. Preheat the oven to 425°F. Line 1 or 2 medium cookie sheets, depending on eggplant size, with foil and spray lightly with nonstick cooking spray or grease lightly with vegetable oil.

2. Remove any stems from the eggplants and halve them lengthwise. With a fork, prick the skin-side of the eggplants all over. Sprinkle the cut sides with salt, place the eggplants skin-side up on the sheet, and bake until wrinkled and soft, about 40 minutes. Let cool slightly then remove the skin and seeds with your fingers. (If removing the seeds is difficult, work them out under cold running water.) Chop the eggplant into large chunks.

3. On a burner or under the broiler, roast the peppers until the skin is uniformly charred. Transfer to a paper bag or a bowl. Close the bag or cover the bowl with foil, a dish towel or plastic wrap. Let the peppers steam until they become cool enough to handle. Remove the stems, peel, and seeds and cut the peppers into 1 to 1½-inch dice. Reserve any juice.

4. In a heavy soup pot, heat the butter and oil over medium heat. Add the onion and sauté just until translucent, 5 to 10 minutes. Add the garlic and sauté 1 to 2 minutes more. Stir in the peppers, eggplant, tomato paste, and stock. Bring to a boil, reduce the heat, and simmer for 1 hour.

5. Using a hand blender (or carefully transferring to a stand blender or food processor in batches), purée the soup. If too thick, add more stock.

6. To make the fricos, combine the ingredients in a small bowl and mix lightly until blended. Transfer to a colander and shake to remove excess flour and any small bits of cheese.

7. Heat a medium nonstick skillet or griddle over medium heat. Add a small handful of the frico mixture. Spread with your fingers to make a 3-inch round. When the cheese has melted and the edges of the frico are slightly colored, turn carefully with a spatula and cook until the bottom is colored, about 30 seconds. Remove and drape the frico, colored side up, over a rolling pin. Let cool and firm. Repeat with the remaining mixture.

8. Season the soup with salt and pepper, transfer to serving bowls and garnish with the basil. Serve with the fricos.

Lentil Soup with "Ham"

serves 8 to 10

M D

In my pre-kosher days I always loved lentil soup with ham or bacon added. Now we have smoked turkey leg, a marvelous kosher alternative to those items and one that tastes absolutely right in this soup. Deeply hearty, this is one of those dishes for which cold weather was invented. Add some bread and a salad and you've got yourself a *meal*.

1. In a heavy-bottomed soup pot, combine the oils and heat over medium-high heat. Add the onion, celery, garlic and carrots and sauté, stirring, until softened but without coloring, about 8 minutes. Add the turkey and sauté, stirring, until it begins to crisp and color, 3 to 5 minutes. Add the lentils and sauté, stirring, for 2 minutes.

2. Add the stock, bring to a boil, cover, reduce the heat and simmer until the lentils are soft, about 1 hour. Season with the salt and serve.

Convert It

To make this a dairy dish, substitute butter for the olive oil, replace the chicken stock with vegetable, and add Parmesan rind, or that of another hard, flavorful cheese, in place of the turkey.

1½ extra-virgin olive oil

1½ tablespoons grapeseed or canola oil

1 cup chopped onion

1 cup chopped celery (about 2 large stalks)

2 garlic cloves, minced

2 medium carrots, peeled and chopped

¾ cup smoked dark meat turkey, cut into ¼-inch dice

2 cups green lentils, rinsed

8 cups chicken stock

Kosher salt

Creamy Artichoke Soup

serves 6

I've always enjoyed artichoke soup, but used to find it a hassle to make. Dismantling fresh artichokes was a trial—and canned or marinated hearts wouldn't do at all. Now we have frozen artichoke hearts, which give this quickly made soup its deep artichoke flavor. For a special touch, garnish the soup with julienned Duck Prosciutto (see page 24).

Convert It

To make this a dairy dish, substitute butter for the olive oil, vegetable stock (page 193) for the chicken stock, and 3 tablespoons of grated Parmesan. Add the Parmesan to the soup before puréeing it. To make this a pareve dish, use vegetable stock in place of the chicken stock.

Geila's Tip

Sieving the soup after it's been blended adds a step, but really elevates the dish.

1½ tablespoons extra-virgin olive oil

1½ tablespoons grapeseed or canola oil

½ cup onion, chopped fine

½ cup celery, chopped fine

1 medium parsnip, peeled, chopped fine

1 garlic clove

12 ounces thawed frozen artichoke hearts, quartered

4 cups chicken stock

¼ teaspoon freshly ground black pepper

Kosher salt

1. In a heavy-bottomed soup pot, combine the oils and heat over medium-high heat. Add the onion, celery, parsnip and garlic, and sauté, stirring, until the vegetables begin to soften, 8 to 10 minutes. Add the artichoke hearts and sauté, stirring, until they begin to wilt, about 3 minutes. Add the stock, bring to a boil, reduce the heat and simmer, covered, until the flavors are blended, about 40 minutes.

2. Using a hand blender (or carefully transferring the soup to a stand blender or food processor in batches), purée the soup. Add the pepper, season with the salt, and serve.

Velvet Chestnut Soup

serves 10

This super-smooth, sherry-scented soup is a major "wow," fit for your fanciest entertaining. A touch of honey adds just the right amount of sweetness, and truffle oil—added to the soup and used as a garnish—kicks the dish into the stratosphere. And it's easy to do. The recipe makes a large quantity of soup, but it freezes beautifully. Follow this soup with roasted meat or poultry.

1. In a large stockpot, combine the margarine and oil and heat over medium heat. Add the garlic, shallots, leeks and celery, and sauté, stirring, until the vegetables soften without coloring, 10 to 12 minutes.

2. Add the chestnuts, 3 sprigs of thyme, and the bay leaf, and sauté, stirring, until the chestnuts begin to brown, about 20 minutes. Add the white wine, bring to a boil, and cook until evaporated, 10 to 15 minutes. Add the sherry and ½ cup of water, bring to a boil, and reduce the liquid by three-quarters, 5 to 10 minutes. Add the stock, reduce the heat, and simmer until the chestnuts fall apart, about 1½ hours.

3. Remove the herbs from the soup, and using a hand blender (or carefully transferring the soup to a stand blender or food processor in batches), purée. Pass the soup through a fine-mesh strainer, working it with a wooden spatula, into a second pot. Season with the salt and pepper and add the honey. Blend again.

4. With the motor running, add the truffle oil in a thin stream and blend. Adjust the seasoning, if necessary, and transfer to serving bowls. Drizzle with truffle oil, garnish with the thyme sprigs, and serve.

Convert it

To make this a dairy dish, use butter for the margarine and use vegetable stock (page 193) for the chicken stock. To make it a pareve dish, use vegetable stock in place of the chicken stock.

Geila's Tip

The recipe directs that the soup be strained before finishing. You can skip this step, but the straining assures a silky mouthfeel that sets the soup apart. You'll get a thinner soup, but one with a "thicker" flavor.

4 tablespoons margarine

¼ cup grapeseed or canola oil

4 garlic cloves

4 medium shallots, sliced fine

3 leeks, white parts only, well washed and sliced thin (see Tip, page 54)

3 celery stalks, cut into ¼-inch dice

Two pounds unsweetened roasted chestnuts, or 4 pounds fresh chestnuts, peeled and roughly chopped

3 sprigs fresh thyme, plus more for garnishing

1 bay leaf

1½ cups dry white wine

½ cup dry sherry

3 quarts chicken stock

Kosher salt and freshly ground black pepper

¼ cup honey

¼ cup truffle oil, plus more for garnishing

Be-All, End-All Chicken Soup
serves 12

When a friend asked me for my chicken soup recipe for a party she was giving, I was dumbfounded. I didn't have one! I'd always potchkeyed, producing soup that people said was great. But a recipe was needed, and being me, it had to be the best. After days of trying every soup-making technique known to Jewish womanhood, and producing bathtubs of soup, I arrived at this one—yes, the best. It's everything you want chicken soup to be—rich, hearty, golden and beautifully clear without having to be clarified.

There's no salt in this recipe, so season it to your taste. The onion skin adds color, but peel the onion if you want a lighter-colored soup. Save the cooked flanken—it adds rich flavor—for making Kreplach (page 57), which you serve with the soup. Or serve this with vegetables, freshly steamed or from the pot. And enjoy!

Geila's Tip

To clean the leeks, trim the root end. With the tip of a knife, slice the leek from both ends leaving an uncut center portion about 1 inch wide. Run the leeks under cold water, separating the layers to remove any grit.

---

4 medium parsnips, peeled and cut into ½-inch dice

4 medium celery stalks, cut into thirds

3 leeks, white parts only, well cleaned (see Tip)

1 medium onion, unpeeled, quartered

2 bouquets garnis (2 crushed garlic cloves, 1 bay leaf, ½ bunch dill, ½ bunch flat-leaf parsley, and 4 peppercorns divided among two squares of cheesecloth, knotted to enclose)

Two ½-pound pieces flanken

One 4- to 5-pound stewing chicken, cut into eight parts, rinsed, any excess fat removed

3 pounds chicken legs, wings, bones and backs, any combination, rinsed, any excess fat removed

1. In a large stockpot, combine the parsnips, celery, leeks, onion and bouquets garnis. Place the flanken on top and top with all the chicken. Add cold water to cover by 1 inch. Bring to a boil slowly over medium heat, 45 to 60 minutes. Reduce the heat and simmer for 1 hour, skimming to remove any surface solids every 10 minutes. Simmer another hour, skimming every 20 minutes, and transfer the breast to a medium bowl. Simmer, skimming as needed, for 1¼ hours more. With tongs or a slotted spatula, carefully remove the remaining chicken and the flanken and transfer to the bowl. (Reserve the chicken, skinned and boned, for chicken salad, or return to the soup. Use the flanken to make kreplach, page 57.)

2. Meanwhile, fill the sink with cold water and add ice. Place a large clean pot in the sink. Line a colander or strainer that fits over the pot with a double layer of cheesecloth. Carefully ladle the soup through the cheesecloth, trying not to disturb the ingredients at the bottom of the cooking pot. When only a little soup remains, carefully tilt the pot to pour it off. (Discard the pot ingredients.)

3. Allow the soup to cool to room temperature and transfer to the refrigerator to chill. Remove any solidified fat from the soup and serve, or freeze in a tightly sealed plastic container.

Onion-Stuffed Knaidlach

makes 12; serves 4 to 6

Growing up, knaidlach—matzo balls—came in one "flavor" only: hard enough to bounce. Do I hear an amen? I determined to do better, especially after I enjoyed light, parsley-flecked knaidlach at a friend's house. The lightbulb really went on after I had soup-filled buns in Chinatown one day—why not stuffed knaidlach? This easy onion-filled version really elevates the traditional matzo ball to great heights, and should become as traditional in your house as it is in mine.

Convert It

To make this a pareve dish, substitute vegetable stock (page 193) for the chicken stock, and canola oil for the chicken fat.

Geila's Tips

You can make the knaidlach ahead of time and refrigerate them in enough cooled broth to cover them. Alternatively, freeze on a cookie sheet, then transfer them to sealable plastic bags for freezer storage.

You can either use chicken stock to make these or seltzer, for lightness.

3 large eggs

5 tablespoons chicken stock or seltzer (see Tip)

5 tablespoons chicken fat or canola oil

¾ teaspoon salt, plus additional

¼ teaspoon white pepper

¼ cup chopped parsley

2 tablespoons chopped cilantro (optional)

¾ cup matzo meal

1 large onion, cut into ¼-inch dice

1. In a small bowl, combine the eggs, stock, 3 tablespoons of the fat, salt, pepper, parsley and cilantro, if using. Add the matzo meal and blend. Cover and refrigerate at least 3 hours or overnight.

2. In a medium skillet, warm the remaining fat over medium-high heat. Add the onions and a pinch of salt and sauté, stirring, until translucent and beginning to brown, about 12 minutes. Drain the onions on a paper towel and set aside.

3. Bring a large pot of salted water to a boil. Reduce the heat so the water boils slowly. (Too rapid boiling can make the knaidlach break when cooking.) Using wet hands, form 1 to 1½ tablespoons each of the matzo meal mixture into a disk held in one palm. Place 1 to 1½ teaspoons of the onion in the middle of the disc, pinch to enclose, and roll between both hands until a ball is formed. Drop into the water. Repeat with the remaining mixture and onions.

4. When the knaidlach float to the surface of the water, reduce the heat, cover, and simmer until tender, 45 to 60 minutes. Remove the knaidlach with a slotted spoon, transfer to soup, and serve.

Kreplach, Boiled or Fried
makes about 50

One of my favorite memories is making kreplach with my grandmother. Their filling was based on regular ground meat. Much later, a girlfriend suggested that I use chopped flanken instead—a brilliant idea, as the meat is super-tasty. Like Bubbie, I'd always made the wrappers from scratch, but when I was pregnant I just couldn't stand on my feet long enough to do the deed. That's when I discovered versatile wonton wrappers, and I've never looked back. Fried, these make an excellent hors d'oeuvre.

1. Fill a large pot with cold water. Add the flanken, and bring to a boil slowly. Skim any solids from the surface. Add the carrots, celery, and peppercorns, reduce the heat, and simmer until the flanken is soft, about 2 hours. (Alternatively, cook the flanken in soup or stock.)

2. Meanwhile, warm the oil in a medium sauté pan over medium heat. Add the onions, sprinkle with a bit of salt (to help the onions release their liquid), and sauté, stirring, until the onions are golden, 8 to 10 minutes.

3. When the flanken is soft, trim the meat from the bone and cube it. Transfer to a food processor. Add the parsley and pulse just until the meat is finely chopped. Transfer the mixture to a medium bowl, add the onions, and season with the salt and pepper. Add one egg and blend; if the mixture doesn't hold together, add the second egg.

4. To make the kreplach, dust a large sheet of wax paper with the cornstarch. Place 4 wrappers on your work surface. Place a teaspoon of the filling in the center of each wrapper, wet 2 adjacent sides of the wrappers, and fold to form triangles. Press the edges firmly with your fingertips to seal and transfer the kreplach to the wax paper. Repeat with the remaining wrappers.

5. If cooking in liquid, bring a large quantity of salted water to a boil. Reduce the heat, add the kreplach and simmer until the wrappers become translucent and soft, 4 to 5 minutes. Don't allow the kreplach to boil or the skins will break. To fry, fill a medium sauté pan with 1 inch of vegetable oil, and heat over medium heat. Working in batches, fry the kreplach, turning once with a slotted skimmer, until they begin to color, about 2 minutes. Transfer to paper towels to drain, season with salt, and serve with the Be-All, End-All Chicken Soup on page 54.

Geila's Tips

You can use the cooked flanken from the Be-All, End-All Chicken Soup on page 54 for the filling. If you do, start making this recipe at Step 3.

The uncooked kreplach freeze beautifully. Put them into barely simmering liquid, or fry them, directly from the freezer.

Extra hands in the kitchen help get the kreplach formed quickly. Here's a case in which I believe in child labor.

3 pounds meaty flanken

2 medium carrots, halved

2 celery stalks, halved

4 black peppercorns

3 tablespoons grapeseed or canola oil

3 large onions (about 2 pounds), cut into ¼-inch dice

Kosher salt and freshly ground black pepper

¾ cup chopped flat-leaf parsley

1 to 2 large eggs, as needed

Cornstarch, for dusting

One 50-piece package wonton wrappers

Newly Minted Pea Soup

serves 6

This is the easiest, fastest-to-make elegant soup *ever*. Start to finish, it takes about a half hour—a little more time if you strain it, which gives it a deluxe texture. But it's equally good unstrained, with some chew to it. Tasting exactly like fresh peas, and with just enough mint to highlight their flavor, this is good hot, warm or cold, for fancy meals or everyday dining.

Convert It

To make this a meat dish, substitute extra-virgin olive oil for the butter, and chicken for the vegetable stock. Omit the crème fraîche, yogurt, or ricotta.

Geila's Tip

Julienned duck prosciutto (page 24) makes a great garnish for this.

2 tablespoons butter

2 tablespoons grapeseed or canola oil

2 leeks, white part only, well cleaned (see Tip, page 54), chopped

½ cup onion, cut into ¼-inch dice

2 garlic cloves, minced

4 cups frozen peas, defrosted under hot running water

3 cups vegetable stock (page 193)

½ cup chopped mint, plus leaves, for garnish

½ cup crème fraîche, Greek yogurt, or ricotta

1. In a medium soup pot over medium-high, heat the butter and oil. When the foaming subsides, add the leeks, onion and garlic, reduce the heat to medium, and sweat the vegetables just until transparent, about 8 minutes. Add the peas, stir, and cook for 2 minutes. Add the stock and the chopped mint, and simmer for 12 minutes. Add the cream and using a hand blender (or carefully transferring the soup to a stand blender or food processor in batches), purée the soup. For a fine texture, strain through a fine mesh sieve.

2. Transfer the soup to serving bowls, garnish with the crème fraîche and mint leaves, and serve.

Coconut-Ginger Squash Soup with Peshwari Challah

serves 8

For years I enjoyed the old standard, butternut squash soup made with cider. Then, slurping a delicious Thai soup one day, I realized that Thai ingredients could bring squash soup to new heights. Thought to kitchen, and here's the result—a marvelous soup brightened with fresh ginger, coconut milk, and served with Peshwari Challah, my naan-inspired bread with dried fruit, nuts and spices. You can serve this without the challah, but if you enjoy bread making, you must try it with.

1. In a food processor, combine the onion, celery, shallots and carrots, and pulse to chop.

2. In a large pot, heat the olive and grapeseed oils. Add the chopped mixture and sauté, stirring, until soft but not brown, about 10 minutes.

3. Add the squash and sauté, stirring often, until beginning to soften, about 15 minutes. (If using the squash purée, sauté for 5 minutes.)

4. Add the stock, coconut milk, cumin, turmeric, ginger and cilantro. Bring to a boil, reduce the heat, and simmer until the squash is very soft, about 40 minutes. (For the squash purée, add and simmer for 20 minutes.) Remove the cilantro.

5. Using a hand blender (or transferring the soup in batches to a standard blender), purée. Add the salt and pepper; adjust the seasoning, if necessary. Transfer to serving bowls, garnish with the chopped cilantro, and serve with the challah, if desired.

Convert It

To make this a meat dish, substitute chicken stock for the vegetable stock.

1 large onion, quartered

3 celery stalks, quartered

4 shallots, halved

2 medium carrots, quartered

2 tablespoons extra-virgin olive oil

2 tablespoons grapeseed or canola oil

2 pounds winter squash, cut into 2-inch dice, or two 10-ounce boxes frozen puréed squash, thawed

1 quart vegetable stock (page 193)

One 12-ounce can lite coconut milk

1 teaspoon ground cumin

½ teaspoon turmeric

1 teaspoon grated ginger

5 large stems cilantro, washed, plus ½ cup chopped for garnish

1 teaspoon kosher salt

½ teaspoon freshly ground white pepper

Peshwari Challah (page 190) for serving (optional)

Fresh Vegetable Minestrone

serves 8 to 10

As wonderful as minestrone is, I'd never found it completely satisfying. Then I discovered the "trick" of putting cheese rind in it. The rind adds body as well as flavor, making a great dish truly super. (For non-dairy versions, see Convert It.) Add some cooked ditalini or orzo, and you've got a stick-to-the-ribs dish that's perfect for cold weather. I also serve this to dieting friends—it's filling but low in calories.

Convert It

To make this a meat dish, substitute olive oil for the butter, chicken stock for the vegetable stock, and omit the Parmesan. To make it pareve, use olive oil in place of the butter and omit the Parmesan.

2 tablespoons grapeseed or canola oil

2 tablespoons butter

2 medium onions, sliced thin

2 garlic cloves, crushed with the side of a knife

1 large carrot, peeled and cut into ¼-inch dice

2 medium celery stalks, cut into ¼-inch dice

1 cup green beans, cut into 1-inch pieces

2 medium zucchini, cut into ¼-inch dice

1 cup cabbage, sliced thin

One 28-ounce can peeled tomatoes, chopped into ½-inch pieces, with their juice

3 cups vegetable stock (page 193)

One 4-inch rind Parmesan, or other hard, flavorful cheese, plus more grated for serving

One 10-ounce can chick peas, drained and rinsed

Kosher salt

1. Heat the oil and butter in a medium soup pot over medium-high heat. When the foaming subsides add the onion and garlic, and sauté, stirring, until translucent but not brown, about 8 minutes. Add the carrot and celery and sauté, stirring, until the vegetables begin to soften, about 3 minutes. Add the green beans, zucchini, and cabbage, and sauté, stirring, until the vegetables begin to soften, about 5 minutes. Add the tomatoes with their juice and stir. Add the stock and rind, cover, reduce the heat, and simmer for 1½ hours.

2. Add the chickpeas and simmer for 20 minutes.

3. Remove the rind. Divide the soup among serving bowls, garnish with the grated Parmesan, season with salt, and serve.

Four-Mushroom Onion Soup with Truffle Oil–Thyme Croûtes

serves 8 to 10

This complexly flavored soup balances mushroom earthiness with the sweetness of caramelized onions, the woody taste of cognac, and suave truffle oil. It began with my discovery of extra sliced mixed mushrooms in my fridge. It was fall, and I was thinking onion soup. A bit of kitchen footwork and—voilà. Well, almost. The addition of truffle oil-brushed croûtes adds to the dish's excitement. Truffle oil may sound la-di-da, but it's a great kitchen investment, something you'll use again and again. You can substitute extra-virgin olive oil.

---

1. In a small bowl, combine the porcini mushrooms with 1 cup boiling water. Soak the mushrooms until soft, about 20 minutes.

2. Meanwhile, in a large, heavy pot, heat 3 tablespoons of the oil over medium heat. Add the onions and sauté, stirring, until translucent, about 10 minutes. Reduce the heat to low, add the thyme, and sauté, stirring occasionally, until the onions are deeply golden, about 30 minutes. Remove the thyme and set aside. Reserve the pot.

3. Strain the porcini, reserving the liquid, and chop the mushrooms coarsely. Heat the pot over medium-high and add the remaining oil. Add the porcini, white mushrooms, shiitakes, portobellos, and sauté, stirring, until the mushrooms are soft, about 8 minutes. Add the cognac, avert your face, and light it aflame with a grill lighter, or a lit tip of a wooden skewer. Add the garlic and sauté the mixture 1 to 2 minutes. Add the wine and simmer until the liquid is reduced by half, about 5 minutes. Add the porcini liquid and 6 cups of the stock and simmer to blend the flavors, 30 to 40 minutes.

4. Using a hand blender (or transferring the soup in batches to a standard blender), purée the soup. If the mixture seems too thick, add more stock. Add 3 tablespoons of the truffle oil in a thin stream and season with the salt and pepper.

5. Meanwhile, make the croûtes. Heat the oven to 325ºF. In a small nonreactive bowl combine the olive oil, 2 tablespoons of truffle oil, and the thyme. Cover a baking sheet with foil and place the baguette slices on it. Brush with the oil mixture and bake until crisp, 12 to 15 minutes. Sprinkle with the salt.

6. Transfer the soup to serving bowls and garnish with the thyme and drops of the remaining truffle oil. Serve with the croûtes.

Convert It

To make this a pareve dish, use vegetable stock (page 193) in place of the chicken stock.

Geila's Tips

You can prepare the soup in advance and freeze it. If you do, don't add any additional stock or the truffle oil before freezing. To reheat the soup, let it thaw, then reheat it, adding stock as needed. Finish the soup with the oil.

1 ounce dried porcini mushrooms

6 tablespoons grapeseed or canola oil

5 cups (about 3 large) onions, sliced thin

3 thyme sprigs plus more for garnish

¾ pounds shiitake mushrooms, stemmed and sliced ¼-inch thick

½ pound white mushrooms, sliced ¼-inch thick

¾ pound portobello mushrooms, stemmed and sliced ¼-inch thick

¼ cup cognac

4 garlic cloves, minced

1 cup dry white wine

6 to 8 cups, as needed, chicken stock

6 tablespoons white truffle oil or extra-virgin olive oil, to taste

Kosher salt and freshly ground black pepper

Croûtes
¼ cup extra-virgin olive oil

1 tablespoon chopped fresh thyme

Twelve ¼-inch baguette slices

Fleur de sel or kosher salt

Fish

Fish

Fresh sweet fish are a canvas for creative cooking. So I'm often frustrated by the limited imagination many kosher cooks give it.

Because fish is pareve, it's usually served as an appetizer for a meat meal or as a main course for a dairy one. That's fine as far as traditional kosher practice goes, but we need to think more globally. There's much more to the kosher fish repertoire. Following the "revolutionary" approach, exciting fish dishes that were once off the table for kosher cooks are now at its centerpiece.

Thanks to the expanded kosher Asian pantry, kosher cooks can now prepare cutting-edge dishes like My Miso Glazed Black Cod, with its enticingly crisp, mirin- and miso-flavored skin and melting flesh, and crunchy Pistachio-Crusted Tuna with Wasabi Mayonnaise. The expanded pantry is also key to haute cuisine-inspired dishes like Chilean Sea Bass with Asian Beurre Blanc, and Sole-Wrapped Asparagus with Hollandaise, a dish that should put that luscious sauce on your kitchen map.

A lot of what's wonderful about seafood can be replicated in kosher dishes. Surimi, a fish-based product that comes in a variety of shellfish flavors, works beautifully in Surimi Crab

Cakes with Red Pepper Mayonnaise. These were once a no-go for kosher cooks and diners, but no longer.

Another conversion approach is to substitute firm, sweet-fleshed fish for the shellfish. My version of the wonderful French fish stew Bourride with Aioli does both. It features firm, toothy fish that provides seafood mouthfeel while dispensing with the shellfish that's usually included in the traditional dish. It also shows you how a dish can be thickened with an oil and egg-yolk emulsion—the aioli, a mayonnaise—instead of dairy products.

Sometimes all that's needed to make a dish kosher is meat-to-fish switch. Salmon with Creamed Leeks uses simply poached salmon in place of the traditional chicken to make a dish that's creamy yet meatless. What's "revolutionary" about this dish, and all the others in this chapter, is a way of thinking. When you expand your sense of what's possible, you free your imagination to create exciting fish dishes where once there were none.

Salmon with Creamed Leeks

serves 6

Ⓓ

This delicious dish gives you all the thrills of French cooking without any of the hassle. You poach salmon partly off the heat—a foolproof technique that's unattended and ensures perfect doneness. The creamy leek bed is equally easy to do, and you can make it, as well as the salmon, in advance (see my Tip). The finished dish is great for company, and gets applause every time.

---

1. In a large sauté pan, heat the butter and oil over medium heat. Add the leeks and season with the salt. Reduce the heat to medium-low and sauté until translucent, stirring occasionally, about 10 minutes.

2. Add the wine, bring to a boil, and cook until the wine has evaporated, about 3 minutes. Add the cream, dill and cumin and simmer until lightly thickened, about 10 minutes. The mixture should coat a spoon lightly. Season with pepper and adjust the salt, if necessary.

3. Add the poaching liquid ingredients to a sauté pan large enough to hold the fillets in a single layer. Add enough water to bring the liquid ½ inch from the top of the pan. Add the fillet skin side down and bring the liquid to a boil. Reduce the heat to low and barely simmer the fillets for 5 minutes. Turn the fillets, remove the pan from the heat, and remove their skin. By the time the liquid has cooled, the fillets will be done.

4. Transfer the leek mixture to a warmed platter. Using a slotted spatula, transfer the fish to the platter atop the leeks. Serve.

Geila's Tip

You can prepare the leek mixture a day in advance, refrigerate it, and, just before you poach the fish, reheat it over low heat, adding additional cream, if needed. If you want to make the fish in advance too, poach and refrigerate it, then bring it to room temperature, or heat it in a low oven

---

2 tablespoons unsalted butter

2 tablespoons grapeseed or canola oil

5 large leeks (about 2 pounds) white parts only, well washed and sliced ¼-inch thick

Salt and freshly ground black pepper

½ cup white wine

1½ cups heavy or light cream, or half and half

3 tablespoons chopped dill

½ teaspoon cumin

Poaching Liquid

1 cup white wine

4 peppercorns

4 large dill sprigs

½ teaspoon kosher salt

6 salmon fillets (about 3 pounds), 1½ to 2 inches thick

Bourride with Aioli

serves 4 to 6

I miss bouillabaisse, which usually contains shellfish. When I discovered bourride, a creamy, garlicky French fish soup that's equally satisfying, I was overjoyed. The soup's richness—and pungency—is supplied by garlic-laced aioli, a Mediterranean mayonnaise that you add to the stew *and* serve with it. This is a great pareve dish, as its texture suggests that cream has been added, but there's none in it.

You can prepare the aioli ahead, refrigerate it, then bring it to room temperature before adding it to the soup. The aioli contains uncooked egg yolks; always use the freshest eggs you can buy from reliable sources, or use pasteurized eggs. Ask your fishmonger for the fish bones and skin called for, but if you can't get them, do without. The soup will still taste wonderful.

Geila's Tips

Always use a nonreactive bowl when preparing the aioli. Metals such as aluminum can darken it. If the aioli breaks or curdles while you're making it, place an egg yolk in a clean bowl and beat it. Beating, add the curdled mixture in drops. Increase the amount added until the mixture has emulsified and thickened.

You can swap unskinned boiled potatoes for the baguette. Place in serving bowls before adding the soup.

Aioli

½ teaspoon saffron threads (optional)

1 cup fruity extra-virgin olive oil

½ cup canola oil

8 garlic cloves

1 teaspoon kosher salt

4 egg yolks from extra-large eggs

¼ teaspoon white pepper

Juice of ½ lemon

Bourride

2 tablespoons extra-virgin olive oil, plus more for brushing

1 tablespoon grapeseed or canola oil

5 garlic cloves, minced

1 medium onion, chopped

2 leeks, white part only, well washed (see Tip, page 54), chopped

1 sprig thyme

1 fennel bulb, sliced ¼-inch thick (see Tip, page 84)

1 teaspoon kosher salt

1. First make the aioli: In a small bowl combine the saffron threads, if using, with 1 tablespoon warm water. Allow to soak until the saffron has softened, about 10 minutes. Strain the saffron and set aside. In a measuring cup combine the oils. In a medium bowl, mash the garlic with the salt. Transfer to the bowl of an electric mixer fitted with the whisk attachment. Add the yolks, pepper and saffron, if using, and beat on medium speed until the yolks have thickened. Without stopping the mixer, add the oils drop by drop. After ¼ cup has been added, add the oils slowly in a narrow stream. When the aioli becomes thick, stop adding the oils and beat in the lemon juice and 1 tablespoon hot water to stabilize and thin it slightly. (If the mixture breaks, see Tip.) Transfer ½ of the aioli to a nonreactive serving bowl, cover, and refrigerate. Leave the remaining aioli in the mixing bowl.

2. To make the bourride, in a medium soup pot, heat the oils over medium heat. Add the garlic, onion, leeks, thyme and fennel. Season with the salt, and sauté, stirring, until the vegetables have softened but not browned, about 10 minutes. Add the tomatoes, saffron, wine and 1 quart of water, increase the heat, and bring to a boil. Add the fish bones and skin, if using, reduce the heat, and simmer 20 minutes. Add the fish, push it gently under the liquid, and poach at a bare simmer until the fish is just cooked through, about 10 minutes. With a slotted spoon, transfer the fish to a bowl large enough to hold it, and keep warm. Strain the bourride into a large clean pot.

3. Meanwhile heat the oven to 325°F. Place the bread on a cookie sheet, brush with olive oil, and toast, turning, until the bread is crisp, about 5 minutes. Keep warm.

4. Using a hand mixer at medium speed, whisk the egg yolks into the aioli in the mixing bowl. Continuing to whisk, transfer the bourride slowly to the aioli in the mixing bowl, and when blended, return to the pot. Stirring constantly, reheat the bourride gently to thicken the soup to a thin

custard consistency, about 7 minutes. Do not allow the bourride to simmer or boil, or it will curdle.

5. Bring the reserved aioli to room temperature. Divide the fish and bread among large serving bowls, ladle the soup over, and serve with the aioli. Alternatively, dollop the aioli on the bread and serve with the soup.

One 28-ounce can peeled plum tomatoes, roughly chopped

¼ teaspoon saffron threads, crushed

1 cup white wine

3 pounds firm white fish, such as snapper, Chilean sea bass, grouper or sea bass, or a mixture, cut into 2-inch cubes, plus bones and skin (if available), rinsed

1 baguette, cut diagonally into 12 to 16 slices

2 egg yolks from extra-large eggs, beaten

Surimi Crab Cakes with Red Pepper Mayonnaise

(P)

serves 4 as main, 8 as a starter

For a long time after I returned to kosher eating, I really missed crab cakes, which were one of my favorite foods, especially in summer. When I was introduced to surimi crab sticks, I was overjoyed. The surimi has the sweet and salty flavor of crab, and works beautifully in these lightly fried cakes. Serve these with Corn Salad (page 137) and sliced avocado in addition to the mayo, and you've got yourself a feast.

Geila's Tips

To make fresh breadcrumbs, remove the crusts from 4 slices white bread, and pulse in a food processor until small crumbs are formed.

Formed to make cakes about 1 inches in diameter, these make wonderful hors d'oeuvres.

One 12-ounce package surimi crab sticks, see Pantry, page 19

1½ teaspoons Old Bay seasoning

2 tablespoons mayonnaise

¼ cup chopped cilantro or flat-leaf parsley

½ cup fresh breadcrumbs (see Tip)

1 large egg, beaten

1 teaspoon mustard

¼ cup scallion whites, sliced thin

¼ cup roasted red pepper (see step 3, page 48), cut into ¼-inch dice

Kosher salt and freshly ground black pepper

¾ cup panko

2 tablespoons grapeseed or canola oil

Red Pepper Mayonnaise (page 197), for serving

1. In a medium bowl, combine the surimi, Old Bay seasoning, mayonnaise, cilantro, breadcrumbs, egg, mustard, scallions and red pepper, and mix. Season with the salt and pepper, and blend. Transfer to the refrigerator and chill for 1 hour.

2. Form four 3-inch patties with the mixture and transfer them to a flat dish. Spread the panko on a second dish and gently coat the cakes on all sides with the crumbs, returning the cakes to the first dish when formed. Chill the breaded cakes for at least 1 hour or overnight.

3. Heat the oil in a large skillet over medium-high heat until hot but not smoking. Add the cakes and sauté, turning once, until golden brown, 6 to 10 minutes. Drain the cakes on paper towels, transfer to plates, and serve with the Red Pepper Mayonnaise.

My Miso-Glazed Black Cod

serves 6

(P)

New York's Nobu restaurant, 1985: Chef Nobu Matshushia's miso-glazed black cod. Me on first taste: *Wow!* I longed to make a kosher version of this great dish, but had to bide my time until kosher miso and sake became available. On that happy day I set to work—and here it is, a dish you'll enjoy often and that's baby-simple to make. All you do is marinate black cod in a simple miso-sugar mixture then broil or grill it. The caramelized skin is delightfully crispy, and really compliments the sweet, moist flesh. Served with Baby Bok Choy with Garlic (page 136)—or by itself with any bitter green—this is stellar dining.

Geila's Tips

This also makes an elegant starter. Just reduce the portion size by half and serve the cod on greens lightly dressed with Asian Vinaigrette (page 32).

I also use this glaze brushed on eggplant when I grill it. Serve the eggplant with roasted meat.

½ cup mirin

½ cup sake or dry white wine

1¼ cups white miso

⅔ cup sugar

6 black cod fillets (6 to 8 ounces each), skin removed

1. In a medium heavy-bottomed saucepan, combine the mirin and sake and bring to a boil. Boil for 1 minute (to cook off the alcohol), reduce the heat to medium, add the miso, and stir until dissolved. Add the sugar, increase the heat, and stir until the sugar is dissolved, about 5 minutes. Remove from the heat and cool to room temperature.

2. Dry the fillets with paper towels and put them in a gallon-size sealable plastic bag. Add the miso glaze, seal and refrigerate for 24 to 48 hours.

3. Bring the fillets to room temperature. Preheat the broiler or place a grill pan or heavy skillet over high heat. Wipe excess glaze from the fillets and broil or grill, turning once, until brown and glazed, about 8 minutes. Transfer to plates and serve.

Chilean Sea Bass with Asian Beurre Blanc

(D)

I was a great fan of Chinese steamed fish with black beans, which were once kosher-certifed but now are not. Thankfully, we can substitute pungent hatcho miso for the beans to flavor beurre blanc, a creamy French sauce that's a perfect accompaniment to the fish. You could use another sea bass, but the Chilean type really complements the sauce, and vice versa. I serve this with wilted greens and a frizzled-leek garnish, but it's great with any simple side dish.

Geila's Tips

The fish and the sauce can be prepared ahead of time. The sauce will hold at room temperature for up to three hours over warm water, or transfer it to a thermos, where it will stay warm for 5 hours or longer. Transfer the sautéed fish to a cookie sheet lined with greased parchment paper. Cover lightly with foil and leave on the counter. For serving, reheat the fish in a 400ºF oven for 4 minutes and serve with the sauce.

Beurre blanc

8 tablespoons (2 sticks) unsalted butter, cut into tablespoons

2 medium shallots, minced

1 teaspoon white wine vinegar or unseasoned rice wine vinegar

1½ cups dry white wine

½ cup sake

1 tablespoon hatcho miso

2 thyme sprigs

2 tablespoons heavy cream

Kosher salt and freshly ground black pepper

1 tablespoon unsalted butter

1 tablespoon grapeseed or canola oil

Eight 6- to 8-ounce Chilean sea bass fillets, skin and blood lines removed

Kosher salt and freshly ground black pepper

1. First make the beurre blanc: In a heavy medium saucepan, melt 1 tablespoon of the butter over medium heat. Add the shallots and sauté, stirring, until soft but not brown, about 2 minutes. Add the vinegar, wine, sake, miso and thyme, and reduce by two-thirds, 6 to 8 minutes. Add the cream and reduce the mixture until thick, about 3 minutes.
Turn the heat to very low and whisk in the remaining butter, adding 1 tablespoon first and then 2 tablespoons at a time, until a light emulsion is formed. If the butter gives any indication of melting, remove the pan from the stove. Season with salt and pepper, and keep warm.

2. In a large skillet, heat the butter and oil over medium-high heat. Season the fillets on both sides with salt and pepper. When the butter has stopped foaming, and working in batches, gently transfer the fillets, without crowding, to the pan. Sauté, carefully turning once, until golden brown, about 8 minutes. (If the fish is more than 1 inch thick, sauté for 10 minutes.) Transfer the fish to plates, spoon some of the beurre blanc over each portion, and serve with the remaining sauce.

Sole-Wrapped Asparagus with Hollandaise Ⓓ

serves 6

Here's a classic pairing—a couple of them, in fact. Asparagus and hollandaise is one of those marriages made in heaven, as is sole served with the sauce. People sometimes avoid hollandaise, fearing its richness or the possibility of it "breaking" while they make it. With my quick, foolproof method, hollandaise will become a go-to sauce in your house. The presentation—the asparagus is wrapped in sole fillets and baked—is also easily done, and looks beautiful.

1. Preheat the oven to 400°F. If using medium asparagus, trim them to 7 inches in length and peel the bottom 4 inches. If using pencil asparagus, trim but do not peel them.

2. Fill a large bowl with cold water and add ice. Bring a large pot of salted water to a boil, add the asparagus, and cook until bright green, 1 to 2 minutes, depending on the type. Using tongs or a slotted spatula, transfer the asparagus to the ice bath. When cold, drain on paper towels.

3. Butter a 9 x 12-inch baking dish with 1 tablespoon of the butter. Bunch 4 to 6 asparagus spears, and wrap with a fillet. Repeat with the remaining asparagus and fillets. Transfer to the baking dish seam side down, sprinkle with the salt, pepper and tarragon. Pour the wine into the bottom of the dish, dot the fish bundles with the remaining tablespoon of butter, and bake until the fish is barely cooked through, about 15 minutes. (The fish will continue to cook away from the heat.) Remove from the oven and let rest for 5 minutes.

4. Meanwhile, make the hollandaise: In a small skillet, melt the butter without browning over medium-low heat. This can also be done in a glass measuring cup in the microwave, stopping and stirring every 15 seconds until the butter is melted. If melting the butter on the stove, transfer the butter to a small measuring cup with a spout.

5. In a 2-cup measuring cup (or a hand-blender container), combine the egg yolks, cayenne, salt and heavy cream and using an immersion blender, beat until the mixture begins to thicken, 45 seconds to 1 minute. While beating, gradually add the melted butter. After half the butter has been added, and the mixture has begun to thicken, beat in the lemon juice and the salt, and add the remaining butter. Alternatively, make the sauce using a regular blender. Adjust the seasoning, if necessary.

6. Transfer the fish to warmed serving plates, spoon the sauce over the fish, and serve.

Fish

24 medium, or 36 pencil, asparagus

2 tablespoons unsalted butter

Six 6- to 8-ounce sole fillets, trimmed, rinsed, dried

1 teaspoon kosher salt

12 teaspoons white pepper

2 tablespoons fresh tarragon leaves, minced, or 2 teaspoons dried

½ cup white wine

Hollandaise

8 tablespoons (2 sticks) unsalted butter

4 egg yolks from extra-large eggs, at room temperature

⅛ teaspoon cayenne

1 tablespoon heavy cream

2 tablespoons fresh lemon juice

1 teaspoon kosher salt, plus more if needed

Pistachio-Crusted Tuna with Wasabi Mayonnaise

(P)

serves 4

My Passover shopping usually takes me to Manhattan's Lower East Side. One year my eyes were bigger than my stomach, and I bought more pistachios than I needed. When I discovered the "extra" nuts I'd stored in my freezer, I immediately thought, *tuna-with-a-crunchy-pistachio-coating*, and this dish was soon born. It's easy and quick to make as the fish takes little time to marinate. Served with tongue-tingling wasabi mayonnaise, this works equally well for company and weeknight dining.

Geila's Tip

I like my tuna rare. If you prefer yours cooked through, bake rather than sauté the fish in a 350°F oven for about 15 minutes.

1½ pounds tuna steak, cut into 1½ x 1½ squares

2 tablespoons soy sauce

3 tablespoons mirin, or 2 tablespoons white wine mixed with 2 tablespoons sugar

½ teaspoons wasabi powder

5 tablespoons grapeseed or canola oil

1 cup finely chopped unsalted pistachios

Wasabi Mayonnaise (page 197), for serving

1. Place the tuna in a gallon-size resealable plastic bag. In a 2-cup measuring cup (or an immersion-blender container) combine the soy sauce, mirin, wasabi and 2 tablespoons of the oil, and blend using an immersion blender. Alternatively, blend in a regular blender. Pour the mixture into the bag with the tuna, and marinate the fish for at least 30 minutes and up to 2 hours at room temperature.

2. Distribute the pistachios on a large plate. One at a time, remove the fish logs from the bag, shake off excess marinade, and roll on all sides in the pistachios. Set aside.

3. In a large skillet heat the remaining 3 tablespoons oil over medium-high heat. Transfer the tuna to the pan and sauté, giving the fish a quarter-turn every 45 seconds, until the tuna is seared and rare inside. Do not allow the nuts to burn. Transfer the tuna to a cutting board, over with foil, and let rest for 3 minutes.

4. Slice the tuna about ¼-inch thick. Fan the tuna on serving plates and drizzle with the mayonnaise, or serve the mayonnaise on the side.

chapter

5

Poultry

Poultry

When people ask me where my dish ideas come from I tell them I look first to the world's best recipes—and they should too. Adapt them, using your "revolutionary toolbox," and you'll create terrific kosher food.

For example, Chicken with Sausage, Fennel and Peas is an almost word-for-word translation of the Italian pasta dish featuring those ingredients minus the chicken. Kosher sweet Italian sausage also adds savor to the stuffing accompaniment to High-Heat Roast Turkey, a dish that in itself relies on the availability of small fresh-killed kosher turkeys for its cooking ease. And the bird's gravy is enticingly enhanced by the addition of kosher port, an ingredient that, together with kosher duck breasts, makes possible a kosher version of the delicious French classic, Duck Breast with Port and Figs. That dish came about when a food-loving friend expressed a wish for a French specialty that was also kosher.

Some adaptations blend traditions. The cross-cultural Asian Slaw with Chicken salutes American slaw dishes, but relies for its tempting dressing on soy and sesame oil, and on crushed dry ramen noodles for crunchy texture.

My take on the French Poulet Veronique, Chicken with Grapes and Mushrooms, is now an everyday classic. Incidentally, it was also my first kosher-dish adaptation, created at college. Back then there was no kosher dry white wine and I had to make do. Now we can use the real thing.

I've also included Cinnamon Chicken Tagine with Prunes and Apricots, a deeply satisfying dish of the Sephardic Jewish table. It's passed through many hands over the years. Now you have my version.

Sometimes thinking outside of the box means thinking close to home. Baked Herbed Chicken is an American classic, a savory, easy-to-do family dish that's stood the test of time. I think of it as a menu building-block, a foundation recipe that will help you establish a repertoire of easy, do-again specialties, the result, I hope, of your own "revolutionary" smarts.

Chicken with Sausage, Fennel and Peas

serves 6 to 8

I love fresh fennel, a vegetable the Italians dote on, but which we tend to neglect. Paired here with chicken and sausage—a great combo in itself—the vegetable really shines. This one-pot dish, perfect for family dining or casual entertaining, owes its existence to newly improved Italian-style kosher sausage. Don't let the number of ingredients put you off; everything goes together quickly, and the result pleases everybody.

Geila's Tips

To slice the fennel easily, trim the stalks from the bulb, and half it top-to-bottom. Core and place each half on your cutting surface and slice it across as you would an onion.

You can prepare this through step 7 several hours in advance. Reheat the dish in a 375ºF oven and proceed.

6 tablespoons canola oil, plus more if needed

1 pound sweet Italian sausage (page 19), sliced 1 inch thick

½ cup all-purpose flour

12 chicken thighs, or half dark and half white meat

7 tablespoons olive oil, plus more if needed

1 large fennel bulb, sliced thin

Kosher salt

2 large onions, sliced thin

12 garlic cloves¾ pound fingerling potatoes, peeled and cut into 1½-inch pieces

2 small lemons

1 cup chicken stock

1 cup white wine

3 rosemary sprigs

4 fresh sage leaves

3 tablespoons fresh oregano or 1 tablespoon dried

2 cups frozen peas, defrosted

1. Preheat the oven to 375ºF.

2. In a large sauté pan, heat 2 tablespoons of the canola oil in pan over medium heat. Add the sausage and sauté, turning once, until brown, about 5 minutes. Transfer the sausage to a roasting pan and reserve the first pan.

3. Meanwhile, spread the flour on a large platter, add the chicken and dredge it. Heat 2 tablespoons each of the olive and canola oil in the pan over medium heat. Shake excess flour from the chicken, add it to the pan, and sauté, turning once, until brown, 8 to 10 minutes. Transfer the chicken to the roasting pan.

4. If the flour has blackened, wash the pan and add 2 tablespoons each of the canola and olive oils. Otherwise, pour off half the remaining oil from the pan. Heat over medium heat, add the fennel, season with salt, and sauté, stirring, until the fennel has wilted, 5 to 7 minutes. Add the onions and sauté over medium heat, stirring, until soft, about 8 minutes. Season with salt and transfer the vegetables to the roasting pan.

5. In the same pan, combine 3 tablespoons of the olive oil, the garlic, the potatoes and 1 cup of water. Bring to a boil and cook until the liquid has evaporated and the potatoes begin to color in the oil, 12 to 15 minutes. Transfer to the roasting pan. (The potatoes won't be cooked through.)

6. Squeeze the lemon over the roasting pan mixture, add the stock, wine, rosemary, sage and oregano, and bake until the chicken juices run clear when the chicken is pierced with the point of a knife, or to an internal temperature of 170ºF., 30 to 45 minutes.

7. Transfer the chicken, sausage and potatoes, plus any larger pieces of onion and fennel, to a warmed platter. Add the peas to the pan and warm in residual heat, stirring, about 2 minutes. Pour the peas and pan sauce over the platter mixture and serve.

High-Heat Roast Turkey with Apple, Cranberry and Sausage Stuffing

servers 10 to 12

My mother never believes that a turkey can be roasted to succulent perfection in about two hours, and declares it a miracle every time the "miraculous" occurs. I just smile—and you will, too, when you try this fast, easy method. The "trick" is to use a 12- to 14-pound bird, which is ample for most turkey-roasting occasions. The stuffing, rich with tart fruit and sausage, always gets raves, too, as does the port-laced gravy.

Geila's Tip

I like to put the turkey seasoning mixture between the skin and the meat (in addition to rubbing it on and in the bird) before roasting it. To do this, just work your fingers between the skin and flesh at both neck and tail ends and rub in the mixture..

Stuffing

6 tablespoons grapeseed or canola oil

¾ cup pine nuts

1 pound sweet Italian sausage, casings removed (page 202)

2 cups chopped onions

4 garlic cloves, crushed with the flat of a knife

5 shallots, chopped

3 granny smith apples, peeled, cored and cut into ¼-inch dice

1 cup chopped celery

2 tablespoons chopped thyme

¾ cup white wine

1 cup apple cider

½ cup dried cranberries

1 pound stale bread, cut into ¼-inch cubes, or one 15-ounce package unseasoned bread cubes (preferably cornbread)

1 extra-large egg, beaten

1 to 2 cups chicken stock, as needed

Vegetable oil, for greasing

Kosher salt and freshly ground black pepper

Fat drippings from the roasted turkey

1. First make the stuffing: Heat 1 tablespoon of the oil in a large sauté pan over low heat. Add the pine nuts and sauté, stirring, until fragrant, 3 to 4 minutes. Remove and reserve. Add the sausage and sauté, breaking it up, until brown, about 10 minutes. Add a little water while the sausage cooks to help break up the meat.

2. Add 3 tablespoons of the oil to the pan and heat over medium-high heat. Add the onions, garlic and shallots, and sauté, stirring, until translucent, 5 to 7 minutes. Add the apples, celery, and remaining oil, and sauté, stirring, until they have begun to soften, 3 to 4 minutes. Add the thyme, wine and cider and stir. Add the cranberries, reduce the heat to low, and cook until the liquid has evaporated, about 12 minutes. Add the pine nuts and stir. Transfer to a large bowl, add the bread, and toss. Add the egg and 1 cup of the stock and stir gently. If the stuffing seems dry, drizzle in more stock and blend lightly.

3. Preheat the oven to 350ºF. Oil a 9 x 12-inch baking dish with vegetable oil, add the stuffing, and cover with foil. Bake the stuffing for 45 minutes, remove the foil, and bake until the surface is crisp, about 15 minutes. Set aside in a warm place.

4. To make the turkey, preheat the oven to 400ºF. Place a rack in a roasting pan and spray the rack with nonstick cooking spray. Add the turkey neck, stock and ½ cup of water to the bottom of the pan.

5. Place the margarine in a small bowl. Add the sage, salt and pepper, blend, and massage the turkey inside and out with the mixture. Place the bird breast side down on the rack and roast for 20 minutes. Give the turkey a quarter-turn so one side is up, and roast for 20 minutes more. Rotate the bird in the opposite direction so the other side is up, and roast 20 minutes. Rotate again so the breast is up. If the breast seems to be browning too quickly, place a foil tent over it. The turkey is done when a thermometer inserted between the thigh and the body registers 165ºF. Transfer the turkey to a cutting board and let rest for 15 minutes. Reserve the roasting pan.

6. To make the gravy, in a small skillet, melt the margarine over medium-low heat. Add the flour and cook, stirring, until the roux is caramel

colored, about 8 minutes. Watch carefully as the mixture can burn quickly. Remove the pan from the stove and set aside.

7. Pour off the fat from the roasting pan and place the pan over two burners. Heat over medium-high heat, add the port, and deglaze the pan. Add enough stock to make 2 cups of liquid and whisk in of the roux. Simmer until the gravy thickens, 4 to 5 minutes. If the gravy seems too thin, whisk in more of the roux, and simmer. If the gravy seems too thick, whisk in more stock.

8. Run hot water through a metal strainer to heat it, and strain the gravy into a sauceboat. Carve the turkey and serve with the gravy and stuffing.

Turkey

One 12- to 14-pound fresh turkey, neck reserved

2 cups fresh or canned chicken stock

4 ounces (1 stick) margarine, melted

8 to 10 sage leaves, chopped fine

1 tablespoon kosher salt

1 teaspoon freshly ground black pepper

Gravy

2 tablespoons margarine

3 tablespoons all-purpose flour

¼ cup port or Madeira

2 to 2½ cups chicken stock, as needed

Baked Herb Chicken

serves 6

If it ain't broke, don't fix it. This quick and easy dish has stood the test of time in my house. Here, chicken parts are baked on a savory onion and thyme-seasoned mixture. The chicken becomes deliciously crispy, and the mixture is served on top. This is a family dish par excellence, one I know you'll add to your weekly menu rotation. Feel free to substitute another herb for the thyme or another acid for the lemon juice.

1. Preheat the oven to 400ºF.

2. In a large roasting pan, combine the onions, garlic and thyme. Sprinkle with the salt, add the olive oil, and toss. Lay the chicken skin-side down on top and sprinkle with the lemon juice. Bake for 30 minutes, turn, and bake until cooked through, 15 to 20 minutes. If pricked with a fork the juices should run clear, or cook to an internal temperature of 160ºF. If the skin isn't crisp, transfer the chicken to the broiler and brown, 3 to 5 minutes.

3. Transfer the chicken to a platter, return the pan to the oven, and bake until the onions have caramelized and the juice is reduced, about 20 minutes. Remove the thyme, spoon the onion mixture over the chicken, and serve.

2 large onions (about 2 pounds), sliced thin

4 garlic cloves, crushed with the flat of a knife

8 sprigs thyme

1 teaspoon salt

3 tablespoons extra-virgin olive oil

12 bone-in chicken thighs with skin, rinsed, any excess fat removed, dried well

Juice of 1 lemon, ½ cup wine or ¼ cup balsamic vinegar

Duck Breast with Port and Figs

serves 6

Several years ago, the French husband of a friend who keeps kosher bemoaned the lack of haute kosher dishes. So for his birthday I "gave" him this delicious dish. It's definitely haute, but also easy to do. Duck breasts with port and figs is one of those meant-to-be combinations. This will *make* your next special dinner, I promise.

1. In a small saucepan, heat the oil over medium-high heat. Add the shallots and sauté, stirring, until translucent, about 4 minutes. And the garlic and sauté 3 minutes. Add the port, stock, all the figs and thyme. Bring to a boil, reduce the heat, and simmer until the liquid turns to syrup, 15 to 20 minutes. With a slotted spoon, remove the whole figs and set aside. Strain the sauce, pressing on the solids, and set aside.

2. Preheat the oven to 400ºF. Heat a large skillet over medium-high heat. Add the breasts skin side down and cook without moving until the skin is crisp and the fat rendered, about 6 minutes. Drain the fat, reserving it for another use.

3. Season the breasts with salt and pepper, turn over, and transfer the pan to the oven. Roast until the breasts are medium rare, about 6 minutes, or 10 minutes for medium. Transfer the breasts to a cutting board, cover lightly with foil, and let rest for 10 minutes.

4. Slice the breasts diagonally and divide among warmed serving plates. Spoon the sauce over them, garnish each with the fig halves and serve.

Geila's Tip

The sauce can be made a day in advance and stored, covered, in the fridge. If you want a super-deluxe dish, use veal stock instead of chicken stock.

2 tablespoons grapeseed or canola oil

½ cup minced shallots

1 garlic clove, crushed with the flat of a knife

1 cup ruby port

1½ cups chicken stock

12 large Smyrna or Calymyrna figs, 6 chopped fine, 6 halved

2 sprigs thyme

Six 8-ounce duck breasts, excess fat removed, skin scored in a diamond pattern, dried

Kosher salt and freshly ground black pepper

Cinnamon Chicken Tajine with Prunes and Apricots

serves 10 to 12

Most cooks know that tajines are sweet and savory dishes, usually featuring chicken, made in a vessel with a conical lid. My version honors traditional Jewish Moroccan tajines, but without the need of a special pot. Flavored with cinnamon, and full of sweet fruit, this is a perfect holiday dish, especially good for Rosh Hashanah, Passover and Tu Bishvat. It's a great weekend family dish, too.

Geila's Tip

This makes a large quantity, perfect for gatherings, but can be halved for fewer diners, or freeze half for later.

½ cup sliced almonds

2 chickens, about 3½ pounds each, each cut into 8 pieces, or 16 breasts, thighs, and legs, any combination, rinsed and dried well

Kosher salt and freshly ground pepper

¼ cup grapeseed or canola oil

2 large onions (about 2 pounds), cut into ½-inch dice

½ teaspoon saffron threads, ground, powdered, or crushed

2 cups chicken stock

2 cinnamon sticks, each about 3 inches long

2 cups pitted prunes

1 cup dried apricots

¼ cup honey

1. Heat a large skillet, paella pan or large roasting pan, set over two burners, over medium-high heat. Add the almonds and toast, stirring, until lightly colored, about 3 minutes. Transfer to a small bowl and set aside.

2. Sprinkle the chicken with salt and pepper. Heat ½ of the oil in the pan over medium heat. Working in batches, add the chicken and sauté until brown, turning once, about 12 minutes per batch. Transfer to a platter and set aside. If the oil or browned bits in the pan have burned, wipe out the pan.

3. Add the remaining oil to the pan. Add the onions and sauté, stirring, until the onions are translucent, about 10 minutes. Return the chicken to the pan. Add the saffron to the stock, and pour over the chicken. Add the cinnamon, bring to a boil, reduce the heat, cover and simmer for 30 minutes. Transfer the white meat to the platter. Add the prunes and apricots to the pan and simmer until the rest of the chicken is done, about 15 minutes. Transfer the chicken to the platter and discard the cinnamon sticks.

4. Add the honey to the pan and cook over medium-high heat until the liquid is syrupy and coats a spoon, 15 to 20 minutes. Return the chicken to the pan, baste with the sauce, cover and warm. Transfer all to a warmed platter, sprinkle with the almonds and serve.

Asian Slaw with Chicken

serves 6

M P

Traditional, mayo-based slaws often miss the mark. This main-dish slaw with grilled chicken gets a savory Asian spin with the addition of a soy sauce- and sesame oil-based dressing. Almonds and crushed ramen noodles—a garnish to keep in mind for other uses—add texture and crunch. I prefer flavorful dark meat for this, but feel free to use white. Fresh napa cabbage is first choice, but you can use packaged slaw for convenience. Minus the chicken, this makes a delicious side. You can make this all in advance; just dress right before serving.

Geila's Tips

To crush the ramen noodles, place them in a resealable plastic bag, seal, and roll a heavy can over them.

Convert It

To make this pareve, eliminate the chicken. The dish works equally well for non-meat-eaters.

Marinade

¼ cup mirin

2 tablespoons toasted sesame oil

2 tablespoons soy sauce

3 garlic cloves, crushed

¼ cup sake or dry white wine

½ teaspoon kosher salt

¼ cup canola oil

2½ pounds boneless skinless chicken thighs or breasts

1 cup slivered or sliced almonds

One 3-ounce package dry ramen noodles, crushed

⅓ cup sesame seeds

Dressing

¼ cup sugar

¼ cup mirin

3 tablespoons toasted sesame oil

2 tablespoons soy sauce

½ cup rice vinegar

1 cup grapeseed or canola oil

1 medium head napa cabbage, sliced fine, or one 10-ounce package slaw

6 scallions, white parts only, sliced fine

1. In gallon-size sealable plastic bag, combine the marinade ingredients. Add the chicken, press out any air from the bag, seal, and refrigerate overnight.

2. Heat a medium sauté pan over medium heat. Add the almonds and toast, stirring to prevent burning, until golden, about 5 minutes. Transfer to a bowl. In the same pan, toast the noodles until golden, stirring, about 8 minutes, and transfer to the bowl. Toast the sesame seeds in the pan, stirring, until golden, about 8 minutes, and transfer to the bowl. Set aside. (You can make this ahead. If you do, cool it completely, transfer it to a lidded container, and store it at room temperature.)

3. Heat a large grill pan or heavy skillet over medium heat. Add the marinated chicken, shaking off excess marinade and grill until just cooked through, turning once, about 12 minutes for breasts, 15 minutes for thighs. Alternatively, broil, turning once, until just cooked through, or grill on an outdoor grill, 12 or 15 minutes. Transfer the chicken to a cutting board, cool and cut into bite-size pieces.

4. To make the dressing, in a medium bowl, combine all the ingredients except the oil. Using a hand blender or whisk, blend, adding the oil in a steady stream until the mixture has thickened.

5. In a large bowl, combine the chicken, slaw, scallions, almonds, sesame seeds and ramen (see page 19). Just before serving, drizzle in the dressing and toss. Transfer to individual plates and serve.

Chicken with Grapes and Mushrooms

serves 4

This was my first "wow" dish, invented while I was at college. I'd have at least ten guests to dinner on Friday nights, and I remember the pleasure of hearing the usual rambunctious crowd go silent after tasting it. They loved my cooking! The dish remains a family and crowd pleaser, enjoyed by kids and adults alike. A simple "bake," you can serve it straight from the oven, warm or cold. I've also made it with a great variety of white-flour crackers, both plain and seasoned, whatever's in the house, and the dish scores every time.

1. On a large plate or shallow bowl, combine the crumbs, tarragon, 1½ teaspoons salt, and teaspoon white pepper, and spread evenly. Add the chicken and dredge on both sides.

2. In a large skillet, heat 1 tablespoon of the olive oil and 2 tablespoons of the grapeseed oil over medium-high heat. Add the chicken and sauté, turning once, until brown, about 6 minutes. Transfer to a 9 x 12-inch baking dish.

3. Preheat the oven to 350ºF. Wipe out the skillet and heat the remaining grapeseed oil over medium-high heat. Add the onion, sprinkle with a little salt (to help it release its moisture), and sauté, stirring, until translucent, about 4 minutes. Add ½ cup of the wine and ½ cup of the stock, bring to a boil to deglaze the pan, and pour over the chicken. Bake the chicken for 10 minutes.

4. Meanwhile, heat the remaining olive oil and grapeseed oil in the skillet over medium-high heat. Add the mushrooms, sprinkle with salt, and sauté until tender and golden, 4 to 5 minutes. Add the remaining wine and stock and boil until almost all of the liquid has evaporated, 2 to 3 minutes. Add the grapes, stir and transfer to the baking dish. Bake the chicken until just cooked through, about 10 minutes.

5. Transfer the chicken to serving plates, spoon the sauce, grapes and mushrooms over it, and serve.

Geila's Tips

If I'm buying crackers for this, I get Manischewitz's Tam Tam.

To make the crumbs, pulse whole crackers in a food processor.

1½ cups cracker crumbs, any kind (see headnote and Tips)

2 teaspoons dried tarragon

1½ teaspoons kosher salt, plus more

¼ teaspoon white pepper, plus more

4 boneless skinless chicken breasts, tenders removed

2 tablespoons extra-virgin olive oil

4 tablespoons grapeseed or canola oil

1 cup diced onion

¾ cup white wine

¾ cup chicken stock

2 cups mushrooms, sliced ¼-inch thick

1 cup seedless green grapes

Meat

Meat

In decorating, I love to mix the old and the new. That goes for my cooking approach too. "Revolutionary" meat dishes are a happy marriage of the traditional and contemporary—and even the trendy.

Take Rib Steak with Herb Wash, which begins with a traditional American favorite—the steak—but gets a tenfold flavor boost from its tantalizing herb wash, spooned onto the cooked meat. This Italian technique is a mighty tool for kosher cooks, as washes are simple to make, require no ingredient hunting, and can be done beforehand. Lamb kufte, a traditional Turkish ground-meat bite, gets a distinctly modern-gourmet treatment with the addition of cilantro; the latter ingredients of Stuffed Veal Breast with Chicken Livers and Prunes are a classic combo that add last-word sophistication to a simple but savory braise.

Kosher cooks should be alert to dishes like Braised Lamb Shanks, a time-honored dish that's nonetheless made a restaurant comeback. A braise that virtually cooks itself, the dish is perfect for food-loving diners, as are Savory Short Ribs, another dish that's been in vogue recently and that kosher cooks should add to their repertoire. I thought of calling the dish Evolutionary Short Ribs, as the ribs used are flanken-style, taken from the same part of the cow as the flanken Jewish cooks traditionally boil or use in soup. Now the cut is company fare.

Having said all this, there are certain culinary "antiques" I honor because they're basic to Jewish cooking. Bubbie's Brisket is one, presented here just as my grandmother Goldie made it—she'd have killed me if I didn't!—and it's deeply satisfying. Another venerable inclusion, but one with much more polish, is Standing Rib Roast. This supreme company dish is really simple to do—fine cuts need little fussing with—and offers dining thrills, both visual and on the tongue. The moral, when it comes to dish making, is everything old can be new again—and should be.

Rib Steak with Herb Wash

serves 4

Nothing beats rib steak for easy, elegant dining. I like to make the best even better, though, by giving the steak an herb finish. Cooks sometimes coat a steak with herbs *before* searing it, and the herbs burn. Here, a garlicky herb wash is spooned onto the steak after it's cooked *and* after carving. This double-wash adds so much flavor, you'll want to use this technique often, particularly for preparing grilled chicken or fish. (See page 196 for an additional wash recipe, but feel free to improvise your own.)

Geila's Tips

The easiest way to determine steak doneness is to press the meat with your finger as it cooks. If the meat feels very soft, like the flesh beneath your thumb, it's rare; if it feels medium-firm, like that same flesh after you've made a fist, it's medium; if it feels very firm, like the tip of your nose, it's well done.

Don't be tempted to buy boneless steaks. Meat cooked on the bone has superior flavor to that cooked with the bone removed.

Herb Wash

½ cup extra-virgin olive oil

¼ cup fresh rosemary leaves

2 tablespoons flat-leaf parsley

4 garlic cloves

1½ teaspoons kosher salt

Two 1½-pound bone-in rib steaks, at room temperature

1. To make the wash, place all the ingredients in a small food processor (or use a hand blender and bowl). Purée, transfer to a small bowl and set aside.

2. Preheat a grill pan or heavy skillet large enough to accommodate the steaks over high heat. Alternatively, preheat the broiler or outdoor grill.

3. Dry the meat well with paper towels. Sauté the meat until brown on the bottom side, 4 to 5 minutes. Turn and sauté until cooked to desired doneness, starting to check after 5 minutes. Alternatively, cook in the broiler or outdoor grill, turning once.

4. Transfer the steak to a cutting board and brush on both sides with the wash. Cover the steaks loosely with foil and allow to rest for 10 minutes.

5. Cut the steaks from the bones and slice the meat ½-inch thick. Brush with the wash and serve.

Bubbie's Brisket

serves 10 to 12

I don't know about your bubbie, but my mom's mom made the world's best brisket—meltingly tender, juicy and flavorful. It was so good I'm passing on her recipe exactly as she wrote it, with the inclusion of packaged onion soup mix—a heresy, I know, but please indulge me. I guarantee great eating. The first cut of the brisket is prettier, but the second from the narrow end is tastier, as it's more marbled with fat. When it comes to brisket, I always sacrifice beauty for taste, and I suggest you do, too.

1. Preheat the oven to 300°F. Place the meat on a plate and rub both sides with the paprika, salt and pepper.

2. In a heavy skillet or Dutch oven, heat 2 to 3 tablespoons of the oil, depending on brisket size, over medium-high heat. Add the brisket and sear on all sides without burning, about 12 to 15 minutes. Transfer to a plate. The brisket will be very dark.

3. Add more oil to the skillet if needed, and add the onions, carrots, celery and garlic to the pan, and sauté, stirring, until just beginning to soften and brown, 6 to 8 minutes. Transfer the vegetables to a roasting pan just large enough to hold the brisket, and top with the brisket.

4. In a large measuring cup combine the wine, tomato sauce and soup mix. Add to the skillet, and deglaze over medium-high heat, stirring, about 1 minute. Adjust the seasoning, if necessary. Pour the mixture over the brisket, adding more wine or water, if needed, so the liquid fills the pan by ½ inch. Cover with foil and roast the brisket until tender, turning occasionally, and adding more wine or water, if necessary, about 5 hours. Let the meat cool in the pan and refrigerate overnight.

5. Remove the chilled fat from the meat and slice the meat ¼-inch thick, or as desired, and return to the pan. Heat, and serve with the sauce on the side.

Geila's Tip

If you like a thicker sauce, purée the cooked vegetables and return them to the pan before the brisket is reheated.

One 5- to 7-pound brisket

2 tablespoons paprika

1 tablespoon kosher salt, plus more if needed

1 tablespoon freshly ground black pepper, plus more if needed

3 tablespoons grapeseed or canola oil, plus more if needed

3 to 4 very large onions (about 3 pounds), cut into ½-inch dice

6 medium carrots, peeled and sliced ½ inch thick

6 celery stalks, sliced ½-inch thick

5 garlic cloves

½ cup red wine, plus more, if needed

One 8-ounce can tomato sauce

One 2-ounce package onion soup mix

Lamb Kufte

serves 4 to 6

Everyone needs a butcher like mine. A few years ago I asked him for a lamb rack, which arrived with three pounds of ground lamb, gratis. What to do with my windfall? I remembered some delicious kufte—spicy ground meatballs—I'd enjoyed in Turkey, and headed to the kitchen. The result of my kufte experiment features pine nuts for texture and cilantro for distinctive flavor. The tahini sauce provides a creamy accompaniment and can also be used as a dip. Serve the kufte with grilled vegetables, and you've got a great informal meal.

1½ tablespoons extra-virgin olive oil

1½ tablespoons grapeseed or canola oil, plus more for brushing

2 cups diced onion

3 garlic cloves, minced

1 teaspoon kosher salt

¼ cup pine nuts

2 pounds ground lamb

¼ cup breadcrumbs, made from fresh bread

2 tablespoons chopped cilantro

2 teaspoons cumin

½ teaspoon freshly ground black pepper

Tahini Sauce (page 140), for serving

1. In a medium skillet, heat the oils over medium-high heat. Add the onion and garlic, season with ¼ teaspoon of the salt, and sauté, stirring, until the onions are soft and beginning to brown, about 5 to 8 minutes. Transfer to a large bowl.

2. Add the pine nuts to the pan and toast over medium heat, stirring, until they begin to color and are aromatic, about 3 minutes. Watch carefully as they can burn easily. Transfer to the bowl.

3. Add the lamb, breadcrumbs, cilantro, cumin, pepper and remaining salt, and combine well with your hands. Form the mixture into 16 football-shape patties, and transfer to a cookie sheet.

4. Heat a grill pan or heavy skillet over medium-high heat, or alternatively preheat the broiler, or an outdoor grill to high. Brush the kufte with oil. If using a grill pan or skillet, brush the pan with oil too. Grill or broil the kufte, turning once, to desired doneness, about 8 minutes for medium. The firmer the kufte to the touch, the greater the doneness. Transfer to plates and serve with the tahini sauce.

Braised Lamb Shanks

serves 4

"Revolutionary" cooking is often about cultural borrowing. Braised lamb shanks are a Mediterranean specialty that brings sophistication to a kosher table. Richly flavored, they make a terrific, hearty meal that's perfect for winter dining. They're also less expensive than their cousin, osso buco, so you can serve them often. Partner with a creamy side like polenta topped with the tomato-rich sauce, and you've got a perfect meal.

2 tablespoons grapeseed or canola oil

4 lamb foreshanks, tied

2 tablespoons extra-virgin olive oil

6 garlic cloves, crushed with the side of a knife

1 cup celery, cut into ½-inch dice

⅔ cup peeled carrots, cut into ½-inch dice

2 very large onions (about 3 cups), roughly chopped

4 tablespoons tomato paste

1 cup dry white wine

2 cups chicken stock

One 28-ounce can peeled plum tomatoes

1 bay leaf

2 sprigs fresh thyme

2 sprigs rosemary

8 peppercorns

1. Preheat the oven to 350°F. Heat the grapeseed oil in a large skillet over medium heat. Add the lamb and brown on all sides, 15 to 20 minutes. Set the shanks aside.

2. In the same pan heat the olive oil, and the garlic, celery, carrots and onions, and sauté, scraping up any remaining meat bits, until soft, about 10 minutes. Push the vegetables to one side, add the tomato paste and cook until fragrant, about 4 minutes. Stir the vegetables into the paste, add the wine, and bring to a boil. Boil for 2 minutes, add the stock, tomatoes, bay leaf, thyme, rosemary, and peppercorns, and return to a boil. Transfer the shanks to a roasting pan just large enough to hold them in a single layer, pour the braising liquid over them, cover with foil, and bake for 1 hour. Uncover and turn the shanks over. Cook until the meat falls from the bone, about 2 hours, turning the shanks every 30 minutes. If the liquid gets too thick, add water.

3. Transfer the shanks to a plate. Strain the liquid into a measuring cup or fat separator and remove the fat. Remove the herbs and return the vegetables to the liquid. For a smooth sauce, purée the vegetables using an immersion or regular blender. Serve the shanks with some of the sauce spooned over and the rest passed in a sauceboat.

Standing Rib Roast

serves 12 to 16

A standing rib roast is royal dining—and a "revolutionary" building block that will help expand your kosher-cooking repertoire. The key is to buy the best meat you can afford and do as little to it as possible. I like to stud the meat with garlic before it's roasted, but other than salt and pepper, that's about all the seasoning it gets. This is also an easy recipe to do: once the roast is in the oven, you can go about your business until it's time to check for doneness. And there's virtually no side dish that doesn't complement the roast, and vice versa.

To prepare the roast, the butcher removes the bones, replaces them, and then ties the meat to maintain its shape. When the roast is done, the bones are easily removed for carving. Save the bones, however; they're great to gnaw on.

Geila's Tip

This is a large roast, but feel free to buy a smaller one; just scale down the other ingredients proportionally.

One 7-bone rib roast (12 to 15 pounds), trimmed, bones removed and replaced, tied, at room temperature

12 garlic cloves, sliced ¼-inch thick

4 to 6 large onions (about 5 pounds), cut into eighths

4 tablespoons sea or kosher salt

¼ cup cracked black pepper

1 bottle dry red wine

1. Preheat the oven to 425ºF. With the point of a paring knife, make slits over the meat's surface and near the bones. Push the garlic into the slits.

2. Spread the onions in a large roasting pan and top with the meat bone-side down. Rub the meat with the salt and pepper, pour over the wine, and roast until browned, about 20 minutes. Reduce the heat to 325ºF and cook to an internal temperature of 120ºF to 125ºF, or 12 to 14 minutes per pound, for medium-rare.

3. Transfer the meat to a cutting board, tent with foil, and let rest for 20 minutes. Remove the strings and bones, slice and serve with the onions.

Savory Short Ribs

serves 6

I always choose flanken short ribs—cut through the bone so each piece consists of a thin meat strip with three or four oval slices of rib bone—as opposed to the single-bone kind. Here, the ribs get a wine braise, from which they emerge fall-off-the-bone tender and deliciously glazed. Served over a vegetable purée, the ribs are yet another cold-weather feast. Feel free to make this ahead of time, refrigerate and reheat; in fact, the ribs are even better the next day.

1. Preheat the oven to 350°F. Dry the ribs well with paper towels and season with the pepper.

2. In a large ovenproof casserole, heat the oils over medium-high heat. Working in batches if necessary, add the flanken and brown on the three meaty sides. Avoid crowding. Transfer the ribs to a plate and set aside.

3. Add the onion, shallots, carrots, celery and garlic to the pot and sauté, stirring, until browned, 6 to 8 minutes. Transfer the vegetables to the plate. Add the wine to the pot, deglaze, and reduce the liquid by half, about 10 minutes. Add the vinegar and sugar, and simmer to reduce the liquid by half, about 8 minutes. Return the meat to the pot, tuck the thyme around it, and add the stock. Cover the pot, transfer to the oven, and cook for 2 hours. After the first hour check to make sure the liquid fills the pot by 1 inch; if not, add more stock. Return the vegetables to the pot, and cook until the meat barely stays on the bones, about 1 hour more.

4. If serving the same day, transfer the liquid to a large measuring cup or fat separator. Let stand for 30 minutes, skim the fat, and return the liquid to the pot. If serving the following day, allow the ribs and liquid to come to room temperature, refrigerate, and skim the fat from the liquid. Simmer the liquid over medium-high heat until syrupy, 10 to 15 minutes, periodically basting the meat with the liquid. Carefully transfer the ribs to plates, spoon the sauce over, and serve.

6 flanken short ribs (about 1 pound each)

2 tablespoons freshly ground black pepper

2 tablespoons extra-virgin olive oil

2 tablespoons grapeseed or canola oil

1 large onion, cut into ¼-inch dice

12 shallots, halved

2 carrots, peeled and cut into ¼-inch dice

2 celery stalks, cut into ¼-inch dice

3 garlic cloves, minced

1 bottle dry fruity red wine

2 tablespoons balsamic vinegar

2 tablespoons sugar

4 thyme sprigs

4 cups veal (page 192) or chicken stock, plus more if needed

Stuffed Veal Breast with Chicken Livers and Prunes

serves 6

I love to braise; the technique produces deeply delicious food that needs little attention while cooking. Veal breast makes a meltingly tender braise that's unexpectedly sophisticated when stuffed, as here, with chicken livers and prunes—a classic combo that I've reworked so neither overpowers the other. Have your butcher make the pocket for stuffing—and serve this to friends who don't mind picking for the most savory bits.

---

1. First make the stuffing: In a small bowl, combine the porcini with 1 cup boiling water and soak until soft, about 20 minutes. Strain and chop the porcini. Set aside with the water.

2. In a medium skillet, heat 2 tablespoons of the oil over medium heat. Add the shallots and sauté, stirring, until translucent, about 5 minutes. Add the livers, prunes, porcini, salt, pepper and sage, and sauté, stirring, until fragrant, 2 to 3 minutes. Add the port, avert your face, and ignite with a grill lighter or match. Cook until almost all of the liquid has evaporated, 4 to 5 minutes. Remove half of the prunes and set aside.

3. Transfer the stuffing mixture to a food processor. Combine with the breadcrumbs and eggs, and pulse until smooth. Transfer the stuffing to a medium bowl, add the remaining prunes and blend. Set aside.

4. Preheat the oven to 350°F. Add 2 tablespoons of the oil to a roasting pan and heat until hot but not smoking. Add the celery, carrots, onion, thyme, bay leaf and peppercorns, and sauté, stirring, until soft but not brown, 8 to 10 minutes. Add the garlic and sauté 2 minutes. Sprinkle with the flour and sauté, stirring, for 2 minutes. Add the wine and reduce by half, about 5 minutes. Add the porcini liquid and simmer to blend the flavors, about 5 minutes. Transfer to a medium bowl and set aside.

5. Open the veal pocket, stuff with the liver mixture, and secure the open side with kitchen twine. Season the veal on all sides with salt.

6. Return the roasting pan to the burners and heat the remaining oil over medium heat. Place the veal in the pan, and brown well, turning once, 15 to 20 minutes. Reduce the heat if the veal begins to burn. Position the veal bone-side down and add the reserved vegetable mixture and stock. Bring to a boil, cover the pan tightly with foil, and bake until a bone can be easily pulled from the roast, 2½ to 3 hours. Transfer the roast to a cutting board, tent with foil and let rest for 20 minutes.

7. Meanwhile, strain the pan contents through a fine-mesh strainer into a large measuring cup, pressing down the solids. Discard the fat. For a chunky sauce, discard the herbs and return the vegetables to the sauce.

8. Remove the bones from the veal, carve and serve with the sauce.

Stuffing

½ ounce dried porcini

2 tablespoons grapeseed or canola oil

3 shallots, minced

8 ounces chicken livers (see page 18 for kashering)

8 ounces prunes, chopped

1 teaspoon salt

½ teaspoon white pepper

3 tablespoons minced fresh sage, or 1 tablespoon dried

¼ cup port

1½ cups breadcrumbs

2 large eggs

6 tablespoons grapeseed or canola oil

2 celery stalks, finely chopped

2 carrots, peeled, finely chopped

1 large onion (about 12 ounces), finely chopped

3 sprigs thyme

1 bay leaf

8 black peppercorns

5 garlic cloves, crushed with the flat of a knife

3 tablespoons all-purpose flour

1½ cups white wine

One 5- to 7-pound veal breast, bone in, with pocket

Kosher salt

4 cups veal, beef (page 192) or chicken stock

chapter

7

Meatless Mains

Meatless Mains

I love meat, but these days I'm apt to crave dishes without it. Other cultures boast large repertoires of delicious meatless mains, and it's time we caught up with them. For the kosher cook, non-meat dishes are especially versatile.

Take Cauliflower Paneer Masala. It's based on spicy Indian masala dishes, but features paneer, a soothing fresh cheese you make yourself. Substitute tofu for the paneer, and the dish is pareve. Cold Sesame Noodles with Broccoli and Tofu also features that Asian specialty, fried for tempting texture. Like so many other "revolutionary" dishes, it owes its existence to our expanded kosher pantry. Thank that pantry as well for Tess' Penne with Blue Cheese, Pecans and Sultanas, a terrifically appealing dish my daughter devised when kosher blue cheese became available.

I'm particularly pleased with the Linguine with Roasted Tomatoes and Zucchini, a pareve dish with a Parmesan-like topping. That cheeseless finish is provided by "pareve Parmesan," a breadcrumb, pine nut and sea salt mixture I devised that has the richness and texture of actual Parmesan. I store the blend and use it for casseroles and other dishes, and you'll want to, too.

Everyone loves a good risotto, and Risotto Primavera, a creamy blend of rice and fresh vegetables, is a star among those satisfying dishes. Most risottos are "meat" because they're made with chicken or beef stock, but this is dairy, as vegetable broth is used instead. It's an example of finding (or devising) a non-meat version of dishes that typically include it—creative thinking that's basic to the "revolutionary" approach.

Eggplant Rollatini—eggplant slices that enclose a meatless filling—is familiar to many kosher cooks. In my version the sauce includes smoky roasted red peppers, a distinctly modern touch that elevates a too-often humdrum dish. Vegetable lasagna, another kosher favorite, is also given vibrant life through attentive vegetable cooking, the inclusion of sun-dried tomatoes, and the substitution of béchamel for the usual mozzarella, which can become stringy.

Did I say these dishes are versatile? They're meant to be mains, but they also work beautifully as sides. It's funny. Kosher keepers often eat "meatless" outside of the house, without considering that they can enjoy even better non-meat dishes at home. Now they can.

Cold Sesame Noodles with Broccoli and Tofu

serves 4

Everyone loves cold sesame noodles, an addictively delicious meal-in-one that also keeps well. Here's my version, which features fried tofu for textural contrast. This is a dish that kosher cooks couldn't make until chili oil and rice wine vinegar became part of the kosher pantry. I serve this a lot in summer—and the rest of the year, too.

Convert It

To make this a meat dish, add diced grilled or poached chicken in place of the tofu and substitute chicken stock for the water.

Sauce

¼ cup sesame paste (tahini)

⅓ cup creamy peanut butter

2 tablespoons soy sauce

1 tablespoon rice wine vinegar

1 teaspoon grated ginger

⅛ to ¼ teaspoon chili oil, to taste

2 tablespoons sugar

One 14-ounce package firm tofu

2 cups fresh broccoli florets, or frozen and defrosted under hot tap water

3 tablespoons grapeseed or canola oil

¾ pound linguine

2 tablespoons sesame seeds, for garnish

1. In a pint measuring cup or immersion blender container, combine the sauce ingredients and 3 tablespoons of water and, using an immersion blender, blend until smooth. Alternatively, use a stand blender. Transfer to a large bowl.

2. Place a clean dishcloth on a work surface. Place the tofu on top of the towel and fold the towel to enclose it. Top the tofu with a plate and add a weight, such as a heavy can. Allow the tofu to drain for 30 minutes. Cut the tofu into 1-inch dice and set aside.

3. If using fresh broccoli, bring abundant salted water to a boil. Add the broccoli and blanch until deeply colored and slightly softened, about 4 minutes. Remove the broccoli with a large strainer and run under cold tap water. Drain and transfer to the large bowl.

4. In a large skillet, heat the oil over medium-high heat. Add the tofu and sauté, stirring, until golden, about 4 minutes. Transfer the tofu to paper towels to drain. Set aside.

5. Bring fresh abundant salted water to a boil in a large pot. Add the linguine, and cook until al dente, following package directions. Drain the pasta, transfer to the bowl with the broccoli and sauce, and toss. Add the tofu, toss and let cool to room temperature before serving.

Risotto Primavera

serves 4

(D)

In the seventies, pasta primavera was a dish you found everywhere. I first discovered it at Manhattan's Le Cirque restaurant, where it was introduced, and made it as soon as the recipe was published, it was that good. Flash-forward to my present wish to create a risotto version. This is it—a wonderful combination of creamy rice and fresh vegetables that everyone loves, even kids. This recipe has a good number of ingredients, but once you've done your prep, everything goes together easily.

1. Fill a large skillet two-thirds full with water and bring to a boil. Add the asparagus, string beans and zucchini, and blanch for 3 minutes. Drain, cool under cold tap water, drain and transfer to a medium bowl. Set aside.

2. In the same skillet heat 1 tablespoon each of the butter and oil over medium-high heat. Add the mushrooms, sprinkle with salt, and add the thyme. Sauté, stirring, until the mushroom liquid has evaporated, about 4 minutes. Transfer to the bowl.

3. Wipe out the pan and add 1 tablespoon each of the butter and oil. Add the tomatoes, 1 garlic clove and the basil, and sprinkle with salt. Sauté over medium-high heat, stirring gently, until the tomatoes have just softened, about 4 minutes. The tomatoes should retain their shape. Transfer to the bowl.

4. Wipe out the pan again, and add the remaining butter and oil. Add the remaining garlic clove, onion and carrot, and sauté over medium-high heat, stirring, until the onion is translucent and the carrot is beginning to soften, 3 to 4 minutes. Add the rice and sauté, stirring constantly, until translucent except for a white dot at the center, 1 to 2 minutes. Add the wine and cook, stirring gently, until the liquid has evaporated, 1 to 2 minutes.

5. Reduce the heat to medium-low and add the stock ½ cup at a time until each is absorbed, stirring occasionally. Simmer until the rice is al dente, about 35 minutes. If the rice is too firm, add ½ cup of boiling water and continue to cook.

6. Add the cream and stir to blend. Add the Parmesan and stir. Add the vegetables and peas and mix well. If the rice seems gummy, add more boiling water to smooth it to a creamy consistency. Transfer to plates and serve.

Geila's Tip

Making risotto isn't hard, but it requires attention. Keep your eye on the rice as it simmers, never letting it to stick to the pan. Make sure the rice is cooked al dente—with a bit of bite at the center.

½ cup peeled asparagus, cut into ¼-inch dice

½ cup string beans, cut into ¼-inch dice

1 cup zucchini, cut into ¼-inch dice

3 tablespoons unsalted butter

3 tablespoons grapeseed or canola oil

½ cup mushrooms, cut into ¼-inch dice

Kosher salt

2 thyme sprigs

1 cup diced, skinned and seeded tomatoes

2 garlic cloves, minced

10 basil leaves, julienned

½ cup minced onion

¼ cup peeled carrot, cut into ⅛-inch dice

1 cup Arborio rice

½ cup dry white wine

3 cups vegetable stock (page 193), heated

3 tablespoons heavy cream

1 cup grated Parmesan

½ cup frozen peas, defrosted under hot tap water, drained

Cauliflower Paneer Masala

(D) (P)

serves 6

Asian cooking is a kosher cook's best friend. With large vegetable-dish repertoires, it offers unlimited good eating to those who want to dine meatless and well. Take this richly spiced cauliflower paneer, a traditional Indian favorite. For years I searched for kosher paneer—a compressed cottage cheese-like ingredient that adds soothing milkiness to otherwise hot dishes—then realized it was simple to make my own. Served over rice, this is a great meal-in-itself that goes together quickly once you've got the ingredients on hand.

Convert It

To make this dish pareve, omit the butter, double the quantity of oil, and use cubed tofu in place of the paneer.

Masala

1 to 2 serrano or jalapeño chiles, to taste

3 garlic cloves

1 inch ginger, peeled

2 tablespoons unsalted butter

5 tablespoons grapeseed or canola oil

1 teaspoon ground cumin

1 teaspoon coriander seed

2 medium onions, roughly chopped

One 28-ounce can peeled tomatoes, chopped, with juice, if needed

3 tablespoons grapeseed or canola oil

1 head cauliflower, cut into florets

1 teaspoon kosher salt

½ teaspoon turmeric

¼ teaspoon cayenne, or to taste

1 tablespoon garam masala

1½ teaspoons powdered coriander

8 ounces paneer (page 194), cut into 1-inch cubes

Cooked rice, for serving

½ cup chopped cilantro

1. First make the masala: In a mini food processor combine the serrano chile, garlic and ginger, and pulse until chopped fine. Alternatively, chop by hand. Heat a large skillet over medium-high heat. Add the butter and oil and when very hot but not smoking add the cumin, coriander seed and the chopped mixture. Add the onions and tomatoes without juice and simmer until thickened, about 10 minutes. Purée using an immersion or regular blender, and set aside.

2. Add 1 tablespoon of the oil to the pan and heat over medium heat. Add the cauliflower, salt, turmeric, cayenne, garam masala, powdered coriander, and toss. Add the reserved masala mixture, partially cover, and simmer until the cauliflower is tender, 15 to 30 minutes. If the mixture seems dry, add some of the reserved tomato juice.

3. Meanwhile, in a small skillet, heat the remaining oil over medium-high heat. Add the paneer and sauté, stirring, until golden, 2 to 3 minutes. Transfer to paper towels to drain.

4. When the cauliflower is almost cooked add the paneer to the pan, toss, and simmer to blend the flavors, about 10 minutes. If the mixture seems dry, add the reserved tomato juice, or water if none is left.

5. Divide the rice among serving plates. Garnish with the cilantro, and serve.

Tess' Penne with Blue Cheese, Pecans and Sultanas

(D)

serves 6

At nine years old, my daughter Tess said to me one day, "Mom, you look tired. I'm going to cook my dinner." And forty-five minutes and a thousand used pots later she asked me to taste this dish, which was terrific. Truly, I thought, the apple doesn't fall far from the—well, you know. While I've made some modifications, the dish remains hers—penne with crunchy pecans in a creamy blue-cheese sauce, whose saltiness is balanced by the sweet sultanas.

1. Bring an abundant quantity of water to a boil. Add the salt and pasta, and cook until almost al dente, following package directions. Drain. Reserve 1 cup of the cooking water.

2. Meanwhile, heat the butter and oil in a large skillet over medium-high heat. Add the shallots, thyme and garlic and cook until the shallots are translucent, 2 to 3 minutes. Add the cream and gorgonzola, stir until the cheese is melted, reduce the heat, and barely simmer until the mixture begins to thicken, 4 to 6 minutes. Add the sultanas.

3. Remove the thyme and fresh garlic cloves, if used. Transfer the pasta to the pan, add the Parmesan and pecans and about ½ cup of the reserved pasta water. Raise the heat and simmer until the sauce is shiny and thickened and coats the pasta. Season lightly with pepper, toss and serve.

2 tablespoons kosher salt

1 pound penne

1 tablespoon unsalted butter

1 tablespoon walnut, grapeseed or canola oil

2 shallots, minced

2 thyme sprigs

2 roasted garlic cloves, or 1 clove, crushed with the flat of a knife

1 cup heavy cream

4 ounces Gorgonzola, or 3 ounces other blue cheese

⅓ cup sultanas (golden raisins)

½ cup grated Parmesan

½ cup chopped pecans

Freshly ground black pepper

Eggplant Rollatini
serves 6

(D)

Baked eggplant slices rolled around a meatless filling is a kosher favorite. My version ups the traditional ante as its served with a sauce that includes smoky red peppers, a great eggplant counterpoint, plus creamy mascarpone. The dish is luscious but light, and can also be made ahead, see my Tip. It's a great family favorite too.

1. Place the eggplant slices on paper towels and sprinkle on both sides with the 2 tablespoons salt. Allow the slices to release their bitter juices, 20 to 30 minutes.

2. To make the sauce, cut the tomatoes in large chunks, combine with the peppers in a medium bowl and purée with an immersion blender, or in a food processor. Heat a large skillet over medium-high heat. Add the tomato and pepper purée, basil, garlic, oregano and 1 teaspoon of the salt, bring to a boil, reduce the heat, and simmer until the flavors are blended, 15 to 20 minutes. Set aside.

3. Meanwhile, preheat the oven to 350ºF. Cover 2 medium cookie sheets with foil and brush with the olive oil.

4. Wipe the excess salt from the eggplant, roll in the paper towels and squeeze the rolls gently to remove more moisture. Transfer the eggplant to the cookie sheets, and bake until tender and somewhat translucent, 15 to 20 minutes. Cover the slices with foil (to trap steam that will prevent the eggplant from sticking to the pan) and allow to cool.

5. Meanwhile, in a large bowl, combine the ricotta, mascarpone, nutmeg and the remaining teaspoon salt. Transfer half of the tomato sauce to a 8 x 12-inch baking dish.

6. With your hands, and using 2 to 3 tablespoons of the cheese mixture, make roll-shapes. Place one partway down from the wide end on an eggplant slice, roll to enclose it, and transfer to the baking dish seam side down. Repeat with remaining cheese mixture and slices. Spoon the remaining tomato sauce over the eggplant, sprinkle with the Parmesan, and bake until tender, about 20 minutes. Let rest for 5 to 10 minutes before serving.

Geila's Tip

You can prepare the filling and/or sauce ahead and refrigerate. Or bake the dish ahead, allow it to cool, and refrigerate. Reheat in a 300°F oven and serve.

---

3 medium eggplants, sliced lengthwise ⅓ inch thick (about 18 slices)

2 tablespoons plus 2 teaspoons kosher salt

One 28-ounce can peeled plum tomatoes

2 roasted red peppers (see Step 3, page 48)

2 large basil sprigs

6 puréed roasted garlic cloves

2 sprigs fresh oregano, or 2 teaspoons dried

¼ cup extra-virgin olive oil

One 15-ounce container ricotta

½ cup mascarpone

⅛ to ¼ teaspoon freshly grated nutmeg, to taste

½ cup grated Parmesan

Linguine with Roasted Tomatoes and Zucchini

Ⓟ Ⓓ

serves 4

This savory pasta dish began with a surplus of tomatoes and zucchini—and the wish to make a pareve dish that had a Parmesan-like finish *without* cheese. The result was the creation of "pareve parmesan," a breadcrumb and pine nut mixture I'm really excited about. The crumbs and nuts provide texture; cheese-like richness is supplied by the sauce, which contains anchovies with their oil. But anchovy-phobes will be happy, as the dish has zero anchovy flavor. I hope you'll devise other ways to use pareve Parmesan, one of my home-pantry basics (see the Tip). And serve this luscious dish often.

Convert It

To make this dairy, use 1¼ cups grated Parmesan in place of the breadcrumb and pine nut mixture.

Geila's Tip

You can make the "pareve Parmesan"—the breadcrumb, salt and pine nut mixture—ahead of time. Store it in the refrigerator in an air-tight container for up to 3 weeks.

Pareve Parmesan

¾ cup breadcrumbs

1 teaspoon grapeseed or canola oil

½ cup pine nuts

2 teaspoons sea salt or kosher salt

1 pound grape tomatoes, halved

6 tablespoons extra-virgin olive oil

1 tablespoon sugar

1 tablespoon balsamic vinegar

3 medium shallots, sliced thin

1½ pounds zucchini, cut into ½-inch dice

1 tablespoon plus 3 teaspoons kosher salt

¾ pound linguini

One 2-ounce tin anchovies with the oil

⅛ teaspoon red pepper flakes

1½ tablespoons chopped fresh oregano, or 1 teaspoon dried

1. First make the pareve Parmesan: Preheat the oven to 325ºF. Spread the breadcrumbs on a cookie sheet, bake until golden, about 5 minutes, and transfer to a mini food processor or blender. Meanwhile, heat the oil in a small skillet over medium heat. Add the nuts and toast, stirring, until fragrant, about 4 minutes. Transfer to the processor and pulse to chop. Transfer the mixture to a small bowl, add the salt and stir well. Set aside.

2. Increase the oven temperature to 375ºF. Place the tomatoes in a small roasting pan, add 2 tablespoons of the olive oil, sugar, vinegar, shallots and 1 teaspoon of the kosher salt, and toss. Arrange the tomatoes in a single layer and set aside.

3. Line a cookie sheet with foil. Place the zucchini on the sheet and toss with 2 teaspoons of the kosher salt and 2 tablespoons of the oil. Place the tomatoes and the zucchini in the oven. Bake the zucchini until tender and beginning to brown, 20 to 30 minutes. Bake the tomatoes, stirring occasionally and rearranging them in a single layer as necessary, until shriveled and their juice has almost evaporated, about 45 minutes. Set the zucchini and tomatoes aside.

4. Bring a large pot of water to a boil and add the remaining kosher salt. Add the linguine and cook until al dente, following package directions. Reserve 2 cups of the cooking water. Meanwhile, in a mini food processor or blender combine the anchovies with their oil, red pepper flakes, the remaining 2 tablespoons olive oil, and oregano, and purée.

5. Heat a large skillet over medium-high heat. Add the tomatoes, zucchini, anchovy mixture, and pasta and toss. Add ½ cup of the reserved cooking water and simmer to thicken the sauce, 1 to 2 minutes. Add more water by half-cups if necessary to smooth out the sauce. Remove the pasta from the heat, add the pareve Parmesan, and toss. Transfer to plates and serve.

Asparagus and Mushroom Lasagna

serves 8

(D)

I've had my share of vegetable lasagnas and most were less than great. Then I enjoyed a marvelous version at an Italian restaurant. The vegetables were fresh tasting, there was no stringy mozzarella, and the fusion of pasta with the béchamel was just right. I wanted more. Here's my version of that dish—vivid tasting and completely satisfying. Feel free to make this with other veggies of your choice, such as artichoke hearts or cubed baked butternut squash. Just be sure to rid them of all excess vegetable liquid before you assemble the lasagna.

Geila's Tip

You can use fresh or dried lasagna noodles (not the no-boil kind) for this.

1 tablespoon grapeseed or canola oil

3 tablespoons unsalted butter, at room temperature

8 ounces mushrooms, sliced thin

Pinch of kosher salt

¼ cup white wine

½ pound lasagna noodles, fresh or dried

12 ounces asparagus, peeled if medium to large, trimmed, cut on the diagonal into ½-inch lengths

3 cups béchamel (page 196), made with milk only

1½ cups grated Parmesan, or more, if desired

One 6-ounce jar sun-dried tomato paste, drained of excess oil

1. In a small skillet, heat the oil and 1 tablespoon butter over medium-high heat. Add the mushrooms, sprinkle with salt, and sauté until soft and all liquid has been absorbed, about 4 minutes. Add the wine and cook until it has been absorbed, about 2 minutes. Set aside.

2. Bring a large pot of salted water to a boil. Add the noodles, and cook until al dente, 2 minutes if fresh, or follow package directions if dry. Drain the noodles, run under cold water and transfer to a clean dishtowel to dry. Return the water to a boil and add the asparagus and cook until tender, about 3 minutes. Drain the asparagus through a strainer, run under cold water to stop the cooking and set aside.

3. Spray an 8 x 12-inch baking dish that can be brought to the table with nonstick cooking spray. Add ½ cup béchamel and spread to coat the bottom of the pan. Add a layer of the noodles, ½ cup of béchamel, ⅓ of the mushrooms, 1/3 of the asparagus, ⅓ cup of the Parmesan, and ⅓ of the paste. Repeat 2 times, ending with a noodle layer. Spread the remaining cup béchamel on top and sprinkle with the remaining ½ cup Parmesan, or more, if desired. Dot with the remaining 2 tablespoons butter and bake until bubbling and golden, 15 to 20 minutes. Let rest for at least 15 minutes, cut and serve.

chapter

8

Sides

Sides

Y ou'd expect "revolutionary" sides to be versatile, and they are. Most are pareve or are easily converted.

Baby Bok Choy with Garlic can, for example, be made in pareve, meat and dairy versions, and each reveals a deliciously different take on this versatile braise. Broccoli Soufflé, a golden-topped pudding that I call neo-kugel, can be pareve, dairy or meat, as can Glazed Brussels Sprouts with Chestnuts. So can Corn with Sage Flan, a silky side that's a perfect mate to any non-saucy fish or meat main. I'm a great lover of savory flans, so I also offer a Velvet Parmesan version, a lusciously cheesy side that's a bit dress-up but also easily done.

Central to the adaptability of many of the sides is my pareve béchamel (also offered in a traditional dairy version), see page 196. Credit nut milk for the non-dairy creaminess of the pareve béchamel and for the sides, like Creamed Spinach, that include it. In my parents' day you'd have to make that dish with velouté sauce—chicken stock thickened with roux—to get the right texture. No more.

Some sides also work beautifully as mains. Middle-Eastern Zucchini Cakes with Tahini Sauce, a favorite at my table, is entrée material for sure, as is Ratatouille Hash when prepared, as suggested, with chickpeas and crumbled feta, or with ground, sautéed lamb. Corn Salad, a toss of that sweet vegetable with peppers, onions and sesame oil-based dressing, can satisfy a hungry gathering with added tuna, grilled chicken or leftover steak.

Simple is usually best, and quickly made sides like Oven-Roasted Fingerling Potatoes and Glazed Shallots prove the point. The potatoes get a rosemary finish, but you can vary the herb to taste. To become golden and caramelized, glazed shallots once required a long oven-stay but, following my method, you get the same result in much less time. Parsnip Purée is an equally quick-to-fix pareve dish that works with a wide range of mains, and trumps the usual mashed potatoes in flavor and healthfulness.

Delicious and adaptable—these and the other sides maximize your options while assuring great eating.

Ratatouille Hash

serves 10 to 12

I was in a restaurant in beautiful St. Maarten when a waiter presented the table with ratatouille served in timbales. It was delicious—and set me to thinking about adapting the usual ratatouille, a vegetable stew, to make it less stew-y. Here's the result, a vibrant, fragrant hash—every vegetable retains its distinctive texture as well as flavor—that makes a perfect meal served with chicken, fish or meat. You can serve it hot or at room temperature.

Convert It

To make this a dairy main course, add a 10-ounce can of drained and rinsed chick peas and crumbled feta. Or, for or a quick, moussaka-like dish, toss the hash with ground, sautéed lamb.

Geila's Tips

Check the bottom of the eggplants you buy. If the pip there is round, the plant is female; if long, male. Male eggplants have fewer seeds.

3 pounds (about 2 medium) eggplant, cut into ½-inch cubes

4 tablespoons kosher salt, plus more

6 tablespoons extra-virgin olive oil

2 pounds zucchini, cut into ½-inch cubes

2 tablespoons grapeseed or canola oil

2 large onions, sliced thin

2 tablespoons tomato paste

4 garlic cloves, put through a garlic press

2 roasted red bell peppers (see Step 3, page 48), cut into ¼-inch dice

2 tablespoons balsamic vinegar

1 tablespoon sugar

¼ teaspoon red pepper flakes (optional)

One 12-ounce can plum tomatoes with their juice

3 tablespoons chopped basil

1. Preheat the oven to 375ºF. Cover 2 medium cookie sheets with foil.

2. Place the eggplant in a colander in the sink and toss with 2 tablespoons salt. Top with a plate and a weight, such as a large can or wine bottle. Let the eggplant drain for 30 minutes, rinse and dry it, and transfer to a cookie sheet. Drizzle over 3 tablespoons olive oil.

3. Place the zucchini on the second cookie sheet, toss with 2 tablespoons salt and 3 tablespoons olive oil. Bake the zucchini and the eggplant until cooked through, about 20 minutes, stirring both after 10 minutes to prevent sticking. Set both aside.

4. In a large skillet, heat the grapeseed oil over medium-high heat. Add the onions, sprinkle with salt and sauté, stirring, until translucent, 8 to 10 minutes. Push the onions to the side of the pan, add the tomato paste to the center, and cook until the paste begins to bubble, about 4 minutes. Add the garlic and sauté the mixture until the garlic is fragrant, about 1 minute. Add the bell peppers, stir, and add the vinegar, sugar, red pepper flakes, if using, and tomatoes with half their juice, and simmer until most of the liquid has evaporated, about 4 minutes. Add the eggplant, zucchini and basil, reduce the heat to medium-low, and simmer, stirring often, until the flavors have blended, about 10 minutes. If the mixture seems too dry, add more of the tomato juice and simmer 4 to 5 minutes more. Adjust the seasoning, if necessary, transfer to plates, and serve.

Broccoli Soufflé

serves 4 to 6

I call this delicious side neo-kugel, that pudding-like casserole usually made with noodles. It has something of kugel's appealing texture, but it's lighter. I make this with broccoli, but you can use cauliflower, too. This is a very versatile vegetable dish that goes beautifully with just about any main course, meat, fish or poultry.

Convert It

To make this pareve, substitute vegetable stock (page 193) in place of the chicken stock. To make this a dairy dish, substitute milk for the stock, make the dairy béchamel, and add 1 cup shredded Cheddar cheese to the béchamel.

1 head broccoli, cut into florets, or one 10-ounce package frozen broccoli florets, defrosted under hot tap water, hand-squeezed to extract liquid

3 large eggs, separated

¼ cup chicken stock

¼ cup breadcrumbs

1 cup pareve béchamel (page 196)

Kosher salt

1. Preheat the oven to 350ºF. Spray a 4 x 8-inch loaf pan or 8 x 8-inch baking dish with non-stick cooking spray.

2. Bring a large pot of abundant salted water to a boil. Add the broccoli and blanch until brightly colored and slightly softened, about 4 minutes. Drain, cool under cold tap water, drain and dry.

3. In a medium bowl, combine the egg yolks with the chicken stock, and beat until beginning to thicken. Add the broccoli, breadcrumbs and béchamel, and mix well.

4. In a separate bowl, beat the egg whites with the salt until stiff but not dry. Fold the whites into the broccoli mixture and transfer to the baking dish. Bake until risen and golden, and a knife inserted into the soufflé comes out clean, 35 to 40 minutes. Allow to rest for 20 minutes. Unmold onto a large plate, or cut into serving pieces. Serve.

Creamed Spinach

serves 4 to 6

(P) (D)

Creamed spinach is an old favorite that everyone enjoys. This pareve version, while deliciously creamy, avoids the excess richness of other versions so you can really taste the spinach. It's a natural accompaniment to a meat meal, though it's equally good with poached fish, or by itself, topped with a poached egg.

1. If using fresh spinach, wash the leaves and, without drying them, transfer to a large skillet. Cook over medium-high heat until wilted, 1 to 1½ minutes. Chop, squeeze to remove excess moisture, and set aside.

2. In a small skillet, heat the oil over medium, add the onion, sprinkle with salt and sauté, stirring, until the onions are translucent, about 5 minutes. Transfer to a medium bowl, add the spinach and béchamel, and stir to blend. Season with additional salt, pepper, and add the nutmeg, if desired. Transfer to a warmed serving bowl and serve.

Convert It

To make this dairy, prepare the béchamel with butter instead of margarine and milk instead of soy.

Geila's Tip

This may be made a day ahead. Allow the spinach to cool, place plastic wrap directly on its surface, and refrigerate. Reheat in the microwave for 1 to 2 minutes, stirring every 30 seconds, or in a saucepan, stirring frequently, over low heat.

2 pounds baby spinach leaves, or two 10-ounce packages frozen chopped spinach, defrosted

1 tablespoon grapeseed or canola oil

1 small onion, cut into ¼-inch dice (about ¾ cup)

Kosher salt

1½ cups béchamel (page 196), made with 3 tablespoons margarine, 4 tablespoons flour, and 1½ cups soy milk

Freshly ground black pepper

Pinch nutmeg (optional)

Baby Bok Choy with Garlic

serves 4 to 6

I like to braise thicker vegetables like bok choy rather than sautéing or stir-frying them. You get all the fresh taste those methods can provide, but less oiliness—and the braising liquid adds another flavor layer. I serve this with miso black cod (page 74), and anything, really, with which a garlicky green vegetable would go.

Convert It

To make this a meat dish, use chicken stock in place of the vegetable stock. To make this dairy, use butter in place of the olive oil.

2 tablespoons extra-virgin olive oil

2 tablespoons grapeseed or canola oil

6 medium garlic cloves, minced

6 to 8 (depending on number of servings) baby bok choy, well rinsed, halved

1½ teaspoons salt, plus more, if needed

Two 1-ounce packages Washington's Golden Seasoning and Broth (page 18), dissolved in 2 cups water, or 2 cups vegetable stock (page 193)

1. In a large skillet, heat the oils over medium-high heat. Add the garlic and sauté, stirring, until fragrant, 45 to 60 seconds. Don't allow the garlic to brown.

2. Add the bok choy and toss until coated with the oil. Sprinkle with the salt, add the stock, and simmer until the bok choy is tender, 8 to 10 minutes. Adjust the seasoning, drain, and serve.

Corn Salad

serves 6

⊕

This delicious—and beautiful—salad began with a bag of corn kernels I'd scraped from cobs served at a cookout. In my house company is a constant. To feed a hungry crowd one day and to use up the kernels, I invented this salad. With toasted pine nuts, onion, bell pepper and a tantalizing sesame oil-based dressing, the salad goes beautifully with my crab cakes (page 72), or with any grilled meat or fish.

1. In a small skillet, heat the oil over medium heat. Add the nuts, and toast, stirring, until aromatic and beginning to color, about 3 minutes. Set the nuts aside.

2. Fill a large pot with water and bring to a boil. Taste the corn; if it's not sufficiently sweet, add the sugar to the water. Add the corn and cook until just tender, 5 to 7 minutes. Drain, and when the corn is cool, cut the kernels off the cob using a large knife. Transfer the kernels to a large bowl.

3. Add the pepper, onion, scallions, cilantro and reserved nuts, and toss. In a small bowl, combine the sesame oil, vinegar, mirin and salt, and blend well. Pour over the corn mixture, and toss well. Serve at room temperature or chilled.

Geila's Tip

Never add salt to the water in which you boil corn. It toughens the kernels.

1 teaspoon grapeseed or canola oil

½ cup pine nuts

6 ears of corn

½ cup sugar, if needed

1 orange, yellow, or red bell pepper, cored, seeded, and cut into ¼-inch dice

½ cup diced Bermuda onion

½ cup thinly sliced scallion whites (from about 4 scallions)

½ cup chopped cilantro

1 tablespoon toasted sesame oil

1 tablespoon rice wine vinegar

1 tablespoon mirin

½ teaspoon kosher salt

Glazed Brussels Sprouts with Chestnuts Ⓜ Ⓟ Ⓓ

serves 6

I'm a great fan of chestnuts, which pair perfectly with Brussels sprouts. Now that kosher peeled chestnuts are available, making this perfect fall side dish is a snap. I prefer "baby" Brussels sprouts, which are about a half inch in diameter. Available around the winter holidays, they're sweeter than the larger kind. If you do use the baby kind, chop the chestnuts smaller than directed.

1. To prepare the sprouts, remove the outer leaves, rinse them and trim the stem ends. If using larger sprouts, cut an X in the stem ends.

2. Bring a large pot of salted water to a boil. Add the sprouts and cook until tender, 2 to 5 minutes, depending on size. Drain and rinse under cold water. Halve or quarter the sprouts, depending on size.

3. In a large skillet, heat the oil over medium-high heat. Add the shallots, sprinkle with salt, and sauté, stirring, until translucent, 2 to 3 minutes. Add the sprouts and wine and simmer until the wine has evaporated, about 1 minute. Add the chestnuts and warm through. Test the sprouts for doneness; if not done add a little water and continue to cook.

4. Add the mustard and turkey fat, and toss to coat the sprouts. Season with salt and serve.

Covert It

To make this pareve, use olive oil instead of the fat. For dairy, use butter.

Geila's Tip

The sprouts can be blanched a day ahead, drained, dried and stored in a plastic bag in the fridge.

Note that I use turkey or other animal fat as a final flavoring. This is a great technique to keep in mind when preparing a "meat" side.

2 pints Brussels sprouts

Kosher salt

2 tablespoons grapeseed or canola oil

2 large shallots, sliced thin

¼ cup white wine

One 4-ounce jar whole peeled chestnuts, cut into ¼-inch dice

1 tablespoon whole-grain mustard

2 tablespoons turkey, duck or chicken fat

Middle-Eastern Zucchini Cakes with Tahini Sauce

makes 25 to 30

P

Like most people, I love latkes, but the traditional kind is a carb-fest—and not exactly light. This delicious all-zucchini version began when I was experimenting with Middle Eastern spices for Hannukah meal making. Tantalizingly flavored, the cakes are accompanied by a garlicky tahini sauce that you could also use for lamb kebabs. The cakes are so good, I've been known to make a meal of them with just a salad and some simple grilled fish.

Geila's Tips

You can keep the cakes warm, if necessary, on the rack on which they drain (minus the paper toweling, of course) in a preheated low oven.

The tahini sauce can be prepared ahead of time and refrigerated. Serve it chilled (as the recipe directs) or at room temperature.

---

2 pounds zucchini, trimmed

Kosher salt

3 small shallots, minced

2 large garlic cloves, minced

½ teaspoon ground cumin

2 tablespoons extra-virgin olive oil

½ teaspoon baking powder

½ cup all-purpose flour, plus extra

1 large egg

½ cup canola oil, for frying

Tahini Sauce

½ cup tahini, well stirred

2 tablespoons orange juice or 1 tablespoon lemon juice

3 garlic cloves, minced

1 teaspoon cumin

2 tablespoons chopped cilantro or flat-leaf parsley

½ teaspoon kosher salt

1. Place a colander in the sink. Using a food processor or hand grater, shred the zucchini and transfer it to the colander (or grate directly into it). Sprinkle the zucchini generously with the salt. Allow the zucchini to exude liquid, about 20 minutes, rinse under cool running water, then squeeze with your hands or in a kitchen towel to remove as much remaining liquid as you can.

2. Transfer the zucchini to a large bowl and add the shallots, garlic and cumin. Taste and season with salt, if necessary. Mix well and stir in the olive oil, baking powder, flour and egg.

3. Flour your hands lightly and form the mixture into 24 rounds about 2 inches in diameter. Flatten the rounds and place on a plate. (The zucchini can be made ahead and refrigerated, for 2 to 3 hours.)

4. To make the tahini sauce, combine all the ingredients plus ¼ to ⅓ cup water in a medium bowl or immersion blender container and blend with an immersion blender until the consistency reaches a thick cream. Alternatively, use a regular blender. If the mixture seems too thick, add more water by the tablespoon, blending after each addition. Adjust the seasoning and chill, if desired.

5. In a large skillet, heat the canola oil over medium heat until a bit of the zucchini mixture immediately sizzles when added. Add the zucchini cakes and sauté until golden on the bottom, about 2 minutes. Turn, press to flatten and sauté about 1 minute more. Reduce the heat to medium-low and cook until the cakes are done through, 5 to 8 minutes, turning once. Meanwhile, place paper towels on a wire rack. When the cakes are done, transfer them to the rack and blot the tops with additional paper towels. Serve hot with the sauce on the side.

Savory Flan Two Ways:
Velvet Parmesan

serves 8

I love the silky creaminess of a flan, so pleasing on the tongue. For years I experimented with savory versions to be served as a side. This was my first success, a cheesy, custard-like dish that perfectly partners any grilled or poached fish. It's also very easy to do. You can also substitute this for the hollandaise in my sole-wrapped asparagus (page 77).

1 cup grated Parmesan

⅛ teaspoon cayenne

2 cups dairy béchamel (page 196), made with 1¼ cups milk and ¾ cup heavy cream, warm

Kosher salt and white pepper

2 large eggs plus 2 yolks

1. Preheat the oven 350ºF. Spray an 8 x 12-inch baking dish with nonstick cooking spray, or butter it.

2. Add the Parmesan and cayenne to the béchamel and blend. Adjust the salt, if necessary, and season with pepper.

3. In a medium bowl, beat the eggs and yolks until well combined. Gradually add the béchamel mixture. Pour the mixture into the prepared baking dish, cover tightly with foil, and transfer to a roasting pan. Add enough boiling water to come halfway up the side of the pan. Place in the oven and bake until the flan is just set (the mixture will jiggle slightly when moved), 50 to 60 minutes. Check after 45 minutes.

4. Let the flan rest for 15 minutes, cut and serve.

Corn with Sage
serves 8

Corn and I are like *this*. I'm always on the hunt for new ways to use it, and this flan is my latest discovery. People who try this flan are often surprised that its creamy texture could be achieved without dairy ingredients, but that's indeed the case, thanks to the eggs and béchamel in it. This super-versatile dish can be served with just about any simply prepared meat or fish.

1. Preheat the oven to 350ºF. Spray an 8 x 12-inch baking dish with nonstick cooking spray.

2. In a medium skillet, heat the oil over medium-high heat. Add the onions and sauté, stirring, until lightly brown, about 6 minutes. Transfer the onions to a food processor, add the corn and sage leaves, and process until puréed. (Some chunks will remain.) Add the sugar, cayenne, salt and hazelnut oil, if using, and pulse to blend.

3. In a large bowl, combine the eggs and yolks and beat. Add the béchamel to the corn mixture, blend thoroughly, and adjust the seasoning, if necessary. Add the eggs, blend, and pour into the baking dish. Cover tightly with foil, and transfer to a roasting pan. Bring enough water to a boil to come halfway up the sides of the pan and pour into the pan. Transfer to the oven and bake until a knife inserted in the flan comes out clean, about 60 minutes.

4. Let the flan rest for 15 minutes, cut and serve.

Convert it

To make this dairy, use dairy béchamel (page 196) instead of the pareve version, and butter instead of the grapeseed oil.

2 tablespoons grapeseed or canola oil

1 medium onion, chopped

One 10-ounce bag frozen corn kernels, defrosted under hot tap water, drained

3 tablespoon chopped sage leaves, stems reserved

3 tablespoons sugar

¼ teaspoon cayenne

1 teaspoon kosher salt, plus more, if needed

1 tablespoon hazelnut oil (optional)

2 large eggs plus 2 yolks

2 cups pareve béchamel (page 196), warm

Freshly ground black pepper, if needed

Parsnip Purée

serves 6

(P)

This couldn't-be-easier purée treats parsnips with the respect they deserve. Whenever I'm inclined to make mashed potatoes, I fix this instead, and everyone is happy. More healthful than purées that contain butter or cream—or both—this is especially good with braised meats, whose rich sauces it soaks up enticingly.

Geila's Tip

Don't skip the parsnip-coring step; the fibrous vegetable interior prevents a creamy result.

2 pounds parsnips

3 tablespoons extra-virgin olive oil

6 cloves roasted garlic

Pinch nutmeg

1 teaspoon kosher salt

1. Peel, core and chop the parsnips into ½-inch pieces. Transfer to a pot with enough cold water to cover them by 2 inches, bring to a boil and cook until tender, 15 to 20 minutes.

2. Transfer the parsnips to a medium bowl and combine with the oil, garlic, nutmeg and salt. Purée with an immersion blender or in a food processor. Adjust the seasoning, if necessary, and serve.

Glazed Shallots

serves 6 to 8

(P)

Traditionally, this dish of caramelized, sweet-and-tart roasted shallots took hours to make. But by glazing the shallots on the stove before roasting them, it's ready in minutes. Crispy on the outside, yielding on the inside, these go with just about any main dish. Use best-quality balsamic vinegar for this.

Geila's Tip

You can make these a day ahead. Roast the shallots for 10 minutes then cool and refrigerate them. Heat them directly from the fridge in a 400°F oven for about 10 minutes.

3 tablespoons extra-virgin olive oil

2 tablespoons sugar

2 pounds shallots

½ teaspoon kosher salt

3 tablespoons balsamic vinegar

2 to 3 tablespoons chopped parsley, for garnish

1. Preheat the oven to 375°F.

2. In a large ovenproof skillet, combine the oil and sugar and cook over medium-high heat until the sugar melts, about 3 minutes. Add the shallots and toss to coat. Reduce the heat to medium and sauté the shallots, stirring occasionally, until golden, 5 to 7 minutes.

3. Sprinkle with the salt, add the vinegar and 1 cup water, and deglaze the pan. Transfer the pan to the oven and roast the shallots until tender for 10 to 20 minutes, depending on size. Transfer to a serving dish, sprinkle with the parsley and serve.

Oven-Roasted Fingerling Potatoes

serves 8

Not every delicious dish needs to be complicated. This savory side of crisp, garlicky potatoes almost makes itself. It's the perfect accompaniment to roast meats, chicken or fish—just about any main item. I like to season these with rosemary, but see other options in the ingredient listing.

1. Preheat the oven to 375ºF. In a medium roasting pan, combine the potatoes and garlic. Add the salt, olive oil and rosemary, and toss.

2. Roast the potatoes until golden, about 45 minutes, stirring every 15 to 20 minutes to ensure even browning. Serve.

3 pounds unskinned fingerling potatoes

6 garlic cloves, flattened with the side of a knife

2 teaspoons sea salt

¼ cup extra-virgin olive oil

Four 3-inch fresh rosemary sprigs, 4 thyme sprigs, or ¼ cup chopped flat-leaf parsley

chapter

9

Breakfast and Brunch

Breakfast and Brunch

Morning appetites require special fare. Bagels, cream cheese and lox have long been that. As beloved as that dish is, though, there's more to a.m. eating. Most breakfast and brunch dishes are dairy or sweet, categories I love recasting to make newly delicious fare.

That penchant is responsible for Crème Brulée French Toast, a luscious cross of the perennial breakfast favorite and the rich dessert, which is particularly appealing when sprinkled with fresh berries. It's also yielded Matzo Brei with Caramelized Apples, a tantalizing elevation of the customary favorite with the bonus of a pleasingly crunchy texture, and Nutella Banana Crêpes with Praline Crunch, a triple-whammy treat that gives the traditional filled-crepe dish new life. My homemade Schnecken are stellar breakfast eating and doable even for novice bakers. The inclusion of maple syrup in their filling sends those rolls heavenward, though just their smell as they bake may be paradise enough.

I'm particularly pleased to present Sheila's Blintzes, the best version of the old favorite I've ever tried. I wouldn't dare mess with these, though I've included a technique for oven-finishing them that makes them easier to do for a crowd, and added a strawberry and blueberry filling variation that will delight your guests. The blintzes also offer cooks the opportunity to explore crepe making, a skill that opens doors to many recipes, savory as well as sweet.

What's new about Omelet Savoyard? Nothing. Stuffed with potatoes, onions and cheese, this frittata-like omelet, a peasant dish from the French Alps, is timeless for a reason. Guests devour it with relish, especially on cold winter mornings. If you haven't made it, you must. A classic you've never tried can be new for you and delicious for your guests.

Nutella Banana Crêpes with Praline Crunch (D)

serves 6

This blowout dish of Nutella-laced, banana-filled crêpes topped with whipped cream and crunchy praline began as a treat for my daughter. But when friends raved about it, I knew I had a crossover hit. Nutella fans in particular will rejoice, as this really celebrates its chocolate-hazelnut splendor. If you're not up for doing the full-dress presentation, make these without the praline or whipped cream. They'll still be great.

---

1. Spray a large sheet of parchment paper with nonstick cooking spray. Chill a medium bowl.

2. To make the praline, combine the sugar, corn syrup and 1 tablespoon water in a small saucepan, and heat over medium-high, stirring. When the sugar has dissolved, boil until the syrup is amber-colored, about 5 minutes. Remove from the heat, add the nuts, stir and pour the mixture onto the parchment paper. Using a spatula, spread the mixture into a thin layer, and let cool completely, about 30 minutes. Break into pieces, transfer to a food processor, and grind to make pea-size chunks.

3. Next make the filling: In a large skillet, combine the butter and sugars and cook over medium-high heat until the sugars have melted and the mixture is bubbling, 3 to 5 minutes. Whisk in the vanilla and rum extract, if using, and cook for 2 minutes more. Remove from the heat, and whisk in the cream rapidly. When the mixture begins to thicken, add the bananas, return the pan to the stove and cook the bananas in the caramel for 3 minutes. Using a strainer, drain the bananas, reserving the caramel in a dish.

4. In the chilled bowl whip the 1 cup cream until soft peaks form. Add the ¼ cup sugar and continue to beat until stiff peaks form. Refrigerate.

5. To assemble the crêpes, stir the Nutella and spread 1 tablespoon from side to side on a crêpe. Top with 2 tablespoons of the banana, and fold by lifting one side of the crêpe to cover the filling and folding the opposite side over the first. Top with the whipped cream, sprinkle with the praline, drizzle with the reserved caramel and serve.

Praline
½ cup sugar
1 teaspoon corn syrup
½ cup chopped pecans

Filling
4 tablespoons unsalted butter
⅓ cup light brown sugar
⅓ cup sugar
1 teaspoon vanilla extract
1 teaspoon rum extract (optional)
¼ cup heavy cream
2 bananas, sliced into thirds, cut into ½-inch dice

1 cup heavy cream
¼ cup sugar
½ recipe crêpes (page 193)
½ cup Nutella, at room temperature

Crème Brulée French Toast

serves 4

⓪ D ⬤ P

I was once served French toast that had a surprising—and delightful—bread pudding-like texture. Here's my version: French toast that owes its tender, irresistible bite and rich flavor to a third dish, crème brulée. All you do is soak the bread in a luscious "brulée" mixture and then double-cook it—on the stove for color, then in the oven to develop texture. Sprinkled with whatever berries are in season, the result is welcomed equally by the young and their elders.

Convert It

To make this pareve, substitute almond cashew cream (see page 17) for the heavy cream.

Geila's Tip

If you want to pull out all the stops—and then some—make this with Chocolate Challah (see page 191).

2 large eggs

½ cup heavy cream

¼ cup maple syrup or sugar

1 teaspoon vanilla extract

Eight ¾-inch-thick slices challah

Cooking spray or canola oil, for greasing the pan

Confectioners' sugar, for dusting

1. Preheat the oven to 200°F. Line a medium baking sheet with foil and set aside.

2. In a large low-sided bowl or large baking dish, combine the eggs, cream, sugar and vanilla, and whisk to blend. Add the challah and press down on it to soak up the liquid, turn, and repeat. The bread will be very soft.

3. Heat a medium griddle or medium skillet over medium heat. Spray the pan lightly with the cooking spray or grease with a paper towel dipped in the oil. Drain half the challah by shaking it carefully over the bowl, place on the griddle without crowding, and sauté until lightly brown, turning once, about 6 minutes. Transfer the challah to the baking sheet. Repeat with the remaining challah.

4. Bake until the custard has set (the challah will be firm when pressed), 20 to 30 minutes. Sprinkle with the confectioners' sugar and serve.

Matzo Brei with Caramelized Apples

serves 4-6

Matzo brei is Jewish soul food. I'm reminded of that when friends invited for brunch invariably demand it. This recipe not only produces great matzo brei but also features an apple-maple accompaniment, based on the caramelized topping of tarte tartin, that makes this special. Diners also love the brei's non-traditional crunchy texture, achieved by pouring boiling water over the matzos to soften them, rather than giving them a soak.

1. In a large skillet melt the butter over medium-high heat. Add the sugar, 1/2 teaspoon of the cinnamon, and the syrup, if using, and stir to blend. Add the apples and sauté, stirring frequently, until the apples have softened and the pan liquid is syrupy, 10 to 15 minutes. Set aside.

2. Bring a kettle of water to a boil. Place the matzos in a colander and pour the water over them to soften the matzo. Drain the matzos and press them against the colander to remove excess water.

3. In a large bowl, beat the eggs. Add the remaining 1/2 teaspoon cinnamon, salt and the matzo, and stir to combine.

4. In a large skillet, heat the oil over medium-high. Add the matzo mixture, flatten with a spatula to fill the pan evenly, and cook until the bottom has set, 4 to 5 minutes. Slip the matzo brei onto a plate and invert the plate over the pan. Cook until the eggs have set on the second side, about 3 minutes. Slide onto a serving dish, top with the apple mixture, and serve.

Convert It

To make this pareve, substitute margarine for the butter.

Geila's Tip

To feed a crowd, double or triple the recipe. Spray a lasagna pan with nonstick cooking spray, spread the matzo mixture in it, and bake in a 350°F oven for 20 to 25 minutes.

6 tablespoons unsalted butter

1/2 cup light brown sugar

1 teaspoon cinnamon

1/4 cup pure maple syrup (optional)

5 Granny Smith apples, peeled, cored, sliced 1/4-inch thick

4 matzos, broken into 2- to 3-inch pieces

4 large eggs

1/2 teaspoon kosher salt

1 tablespoon grapeseed or canola oil

Schnecken

makes 12

(D)

Homemade *schnecken*—the name is German for snails, whose shell-shapes the rolls imitate—excite everyone. As they bake, they fill the house with the scent of butter, cinnamon and caramelized sugar—and then comes that first bite! My version features maple syrup in the nut-strewn topping, which takes the rolls to a whole new level. Even novice bakers enjoy making these rolls, as no special skills are required.

Dough

One ¼-ounce package active dry yeast

¼ cup plus 1 tablespoon sugar

3 to 3½ cups bread flour, as needed

½ teaspoon kosher salt

6 tablespoons unsalted butter, melted

½ cup milk

½ cup heavy cream

2 large eggs

Topping

10 tablespoons unsalted butter, softened

¼ cup light brown sugar

⅓ cup pure maple syrup

1 cup chopped walnuts, pecans and/or skinless hazelnuts

Filling

1½ cups light brown sugar

¼ cup sugar

1 tablespoon cinnamon

Wash

1 large egg

2 tablespoons heavy cream

1. First make the dough: In a small bowl or measuring cup, combine the yeast and the 1 tablespoon sugar with ¼ cup warm (105°F) water. Stir and let rise until the mixture has doubled in size, 10 to 20 minutes.

2. In the bowl of a standing mixer fitted with the paddle attachment, combine the flour, salt and remaining ¼ cup sugar. In a small bowl, combine the butter, milk, cream and eggs, and blend. Add the liquid and yeast mixtures to the mixer bowl and mix at medium speed until well combined. Replace the paddle with the dough hook and knead for 5 minutes, adding more flour if necessary to achieve a smooth, elastic dough. Transfer the dough to an oiled medium bowl, cover with plastic wrap, and let rise until doubled in bulk, about 60 minutes.

3. Meanwhile, make the topping: Grease a 9 x 13-inch baking dish. In a small bowl, combine the butter and brown sugar. Beat in the syrup and nuts. Transfer to the baking dish, and spread evenly.

4. Next, make the filling: In a small bowl, combine the sugars and the cinnamon, mix, and toss with the nuts. Set aside.

5. Preheat the oven to 350°F. Punch down the dough in the bowl and let rest for 10 minutes.

6. Turn the dough onto a work surface and roll into a 9 x 18-inch rectangle. In a small bowl, combine the wash ingredients, and brush over the dough. Sprinkle evenly with the filling. Starting with the long end nearest you, roll the dough jelly roll-fashion. Slice the roll into 1½-inch pieces and arrange on top of the topping in the baking dish, spacing the pieces evenly and leaving sufficient room between them to allow them to rise. Set aside for 20 minutes.

7. Meanwhile, cover an 11 x 17-inch baking sheet with parchment paper and set aside. Bake the schnecken until golden, 20 to 25 minutes, and invert onto the parchment. Scrape out any topping that remains in the dish and distribute evenly over the schnecken. Let cool before serving.

Omelet Savoyard

serves 4

This French classic—a frittata-like omelet filled with potatoes, onions and cheese that originated in the peasant kitchens of Savoy—may be the ultimate brunch dish. People love its hearty flavor—and it's easily made, as it's all done in a single pan. I like to serve the omelet moist, but you can cook it to the texture you prefer. Offer this with a salad of mixed field greens and you'll be in business.

Geila's Tips

You can prepare the potatoes and onions in advance and refrigerate them. Before making the omelet, bring them to room temperature.

If you don't have a skillet with an ovenproof handle, wrap your handle with foil before putting it in the oven.

---

8 ounces Yukon gold potatoes, unpeeled, cut into ¼-inch dice

2 teaspoons kosher salt, plus more

2 tablespoons grapeseed or canola oil

1 tablespoon unsalted butter

1 onion, sliced thin

8 large eggs

3 tablespoons heavy cream (optional)

¾ cup shredded hard cheese, such as Swiss or Gruyère

¾ cup semi-soft cheese, such as raclette or havarti

2 tablespoons chopped parsley (optional)

1. In a 9-inch skillet with an ovenproof handle, combine the potatoes, 1 cup water and 1 teaspoon salt. Bring to a boil over medium-high heat and simmer until fork tender, 8 to 10 minutes. Drain the potatoes and transfer to a plate.

2. In the same skillet, heat 1 tablespoon of the oil and the butter. When the butter stops foaming, add the onion, sprinkle with a pinch of salt, and sauté until the onions are golden, 5 to 7 minutes. Return the potatoes to the pan to reheat, then transfer everything to a plate, and set aside.

3. In a medium bowl, beat the eggs with 1 teaspoon of salt until blended. Add the cream, if using.

4. Position an oven rack to the top third of the oven. Preheat the broiler.

5. In the pan, heat the remaining oil over medium-high until hot but not smoking. Add half the egg mixture, swirl and cook the eggs until three-quarters done to your liking, about 3 minutes for still runny. Distribute the hard cheese over the eggs, leaving a half-inch border. Spread the potato mixture over, top with the soft cheese and pour the remaining egg mixture over. Place the pan under the broiler and cook for 3 minutes, or 4 to 5 minutes if you like your eggs dry. Invert the omelet onto a serving dish, cover with foil, and let rest for 5 minutes. Sprinkle with the parsley, if using, cut into wedges and serve.

Sheila's Blintzes

makes 16

(D)

Once a year my normally diet-conscious family gathers on Shavuot, the harvest holiday that celebrates the giving of the Torah, for a calorie-defying blintz debauch. This version of those cheese-filled crêpes is from my mother's friend Sheila, whose blintzes are the world's best. My contributions are a technique for finishing the blintzes in the oven, which makes serving them for a gathering easy (see the Tip), and a filling variation featuring strawberries or blueberries. Passed with a variety of accompaniments, these are heavenly.

1. Place a colander in a sink. Place the farmer's cheese in the colander and let drain for 15 minutes. Double a large sheet of paper towels, turn the cheese onto it, enclose it in the towels, and press it to extract more liquid.

2. In a medium bowl, combine the farmer's cheese, cream cheese, sugar, egg, vanilla, and zest and wheat germ, if using. Beat until the mixture is fairly smooth.

3. Place a crêpe, darker side up, on a work surface. Place 2 tablespoons of the filling in the center. To form the blintz, fold the nearest side over to cover the filling, fold the sides toward the center, then fold again to "close" the blintz. Transfer to a dish, seam side down. Repeat with the remaining crêpes and filling.

4. In a medium skillet, heat the oil and butter over medium until the butter stops foaming. Working in batches, and adding more oil and butter if needed, fry the blintzes seam side down until golden, about 3 minutes. Turn and repeat on the second side. Transfer the blintzes to paper towels as they're cooked. (You can keep them warm in the oven, if necessary.)

5. Transfer the blintzes to serving plates. Dust with confectioners' sugar, if using, and serve with the accompaniment(s) of choice.

Variation:

For strawberry or blueberry blintzes, make the filling without the sugar. In a glass measuring cup, melt ½ cup strawberry or blueberry jam in the microwave for 30 seconds. Alternatively, melt it in a small saucepan over low heat. Let the jam cool before mixing into the filling. For a sweeter filling, add sugar by teaspoons to taste. Form the blintzes and proceed as above.

Geila's Tip

To make these for a crowd, line a cookie sheet with parchment paper and brush with 2 tablespoons of melted butter. Place the formed blintzes on it seam side down, and brush the tops with 2 more tablespoons of melted butter. Bake in a preheated 350°F oven until golden, about 10 minutes.

1 pound unsalted farmer's cheese

4 ounces cream cheese

¼ cup sugar

1 large egg

1 tablespoon vanilla

1 tablespoon grated lemon zest (optional)

1 cup wheat germ (optional)

1 recipe crêpes (page 193)

1 tablespoon grapeseed or canola oil, plus more, if needed

1 tablespoon unsalted butter, plus more, if needed

Confectioners' sugar, for dusting (optional)

Sour cream, maple syrup and/or fresh fruit, such as berries or sliced peaches, for serving

chapter

10

Sweets

Sweets

The kosher sweet repertoire is richly diverse. Even so, kosher dessert makers can feel their options are limited. How to create great non-dairy sweets from recipes that depend on milk, butter or cream? How to make Passover desserts that deliver all the satisfaction of their everyday counterparts? "Revolutionary" thinking can help!

For converting dairy sweets to non-dairy ones, nut milks rule. Since their kosher certification, we no longer need rely on ersatz "creams" to provide pareve creaminess. Similar in their fat and protein profiles to dairy milks, nut milks' natural sweetness also makes them ideal for dairy dessert recasting. For example, coconut milk helps make a lusciously creamy pareve version of Crème Brûlée that's every bit as delicious as the dairy kind; it performs similarly to make the filling of Macadamia Raspberry Tart alluringly lush.

Margarine has had a loveless career, but works beautifully in the pareve version of Everyday Banana Cake, a household staple; in Maple Pecan Pie, a traditional favorite enhanced with maple syrup; and in Almond Crescents, terrific pareve bites that people can't get enough of.

Eggs are central to sweet making—they bind, moisten and act as a leavening, a talent Passover bakers put to good use. Eggs make Blueberry Lemon-Curd Sponge Cake light and are responsible for French Macarons, an elegant sandwich cookie that can be tricky to make, but which I've demystified for home cooks. Egg white-based Chocolate Walnut Meringues take the usual Passover meringue cookie to a much higher place, and can be fun to make with kids.

Speaking of chocolate, I couldn't do this chapter without including really serious chocolate desserts. Chocolate Soufflé Roll with Hazelnut Cream, and Lava Cakes, with their molten chocolate centers, are guaranteed to make chocolate lovers very, very happy. The roll was created for Passover and should definitely settle the question of whether Passover desserts can be as tempting as the everyday kind. They can.

Lava Cakes

serves 6 to 8

Who doesn't love rich chocolate cake with a gooey chocolate center? There's just enough flour in these aptly named ramekin-size cakes to give them a bit of body, so you know you're eating cake, not pudding. Otherwise, they're molten lusciousness. Finish them with just a sprinkling of confectioners' sugar, or serve them with whipped cream, ice cream, or any complementary dessert sauce.

Covert It

To make these pareve, substitute margarine for the butter.

Geila's Tip

These can be assembled, frozen and baked later, directly from the freezer. Just add two minutes to the indicated baking time.

5 ounces dark chocolate

10 tablespoons unsalted butter

3 large eggs plus 3 yolks

1 cup confectioners' sugar

⅓ cup all-purpose flour

1. Preheat the oven to 450°F. Spray eight 4-ounce or six 6-ounce ramekins with nonstick cooking spray. Set aside.

2. In a medium glass bowl, combine the chocolate and butter and melt in the microwave, stirring every 30 seconds, for about 1½ minutes. Stir until smooth and set aside.

3. In the bowl of a standing mixer, or in a medium bowl, combine the eggs and yolks, and beat at medium speed, or by hand, until well combined, about 2 minutes if using a mixer. Add the sugar and beat until thick, about 3 minutes. Add the chocolate mixture, beat, add the flour, and beat until just combined. Spoon the mixture into the ramekins, place on a cookie sheet, and bake until set but still soft in the middle, 8 to 10 minutes for 4-ounce ramekins, 10 to 12 minutes for 6-ounce. Cool for 1 minute, run a knife around the edges of the cakes, and invert onto dessert plates, and serve with an accompaniment, if using.

Everyday Banana Cake

serves 10 to 12

This banana cake is so popular in my house, I always have one in the freezer. Beautifully moist and with a pleasingly dense crumb, this walnut-studded version is the best I've tried. It's perfect for everyday snacking, or as a finish to a rich meal.

1. Cut a piece of parchment paper to fit a 9-inch cake pan and grease the paper. Set aside.

2. Sift together into a medium bowl the flour, baking powder, baking soda and salt. Set aside.

3. In the bowl of a stand mixer combine the sugar and butter and beat at medium speed until creamed, 2 to 3 minutes. Add the vanilla and blend. Add the eggs, reduce the speed to low, and add the flour mixture gradually, and beat just until completely incorporated. Do not over-beat. Add the bananas and blend. Stir in the chopped walnuts, if using, and pour the batter into the pan. Arrange the walnut haves in a flower-petal pattern, 6 in the center and 12 around the cake's edge.

4. Bake until a skewer inserted in the middle of the cake comes out clean, 45 to 60 minutes. If the top of the cake appears to be browning too quickly after 30 minutes, cover it loosely with foil. Run a knife around the cake's edge, invert onto a rack, and invert again on a second rack so the top is up. Cool before serving.

Convert It

To make this pareve, substitute margarine for the butter.

Geila's Tip

If you've got bananas on hand that are too ripe to eat, freeze them. When you've accumulated enough, defrost and drain them, then use them to make this cake.

2 cups flour

¾ teaspoon baking powder

1 teaspoon baking soda

Pinch salt

1 cup sugar

10 tablespoons unsweetened butter

1 tablespoon vanilla

2 large eggs

4 large or 5 medium very ripe bananas, mashed

¾ cup chopped walnuts or pecans, plus 18 haves (optional)

Blueberry Lemon-Curd Sponge Cake

serves about 12

Like many kosher cooks, I've made my share of sponge cakes, so-so, good and better. This one evolved from my wish to make an exceptional holiday version. My potchkying began with the addition of lemon zest. A year later I added a layer of rich and tangy lemon curd, followed, a year after that, by a blueberry garnish. I think you'll find the result of my tinkering as special as I do. This perfected Passover dessert is also great for tea, a summer lunch or a picnic.

1. Preheat the oven to 350ºF. Grease a 10-inch tube pan with a removable bottom.

2. In a medium bowl, beat the egg whites until stiff but not dry. Set aside.

3. In the bowl of a stand mixer combine the yolks and sugar and beat at high speed until smooth and fluffy. Add the lemon juice and combine. Add the cake meal, starch, salt, and lemon zest and blend. Remove the bowl from the mixer and fold in the whites 1/3 at a time. Pour the batter into the prepared tube pan and bake until a skewer inserted in the center comes out clean, about 60 minutes. Cool for 10 minutes, run a knife around the cake, and remove on the pan base. Finish cooling.

4. Meanwhile make the lemon curd: In a mini-food processor combine the sugar and lemon zest and pulse until combined. Fill a small saucepan 2/3 full of water and bring to a simmer over medium heat. In a nonreactive bowl, combine the yolks, sugar and zest mixture, lemon juice and starch, place over but not touching the water, and whisk until it thickens to the consistency of a loose pudding, about 4 minutes. Remove the mixture from the heat and add the margarine, stirring to blend. Strain the mixture into a small bowl, cover with plastic wrap so it touches the top of the curd, and refrigerate for at least 2 hours, or overnight.

5. Make a simple syrup: In a small saucepan combine 3/4 cup sugar and 3/4 cup water and bring to a boil over medium heat, stirring until the sugar dissolves completely, about 3 minutes. Alternatively, combine the sugar and water in a pint measuring cup, and microwave until the syrup forms, stirring the mixture every 30 seconds, about 3 minutes. Chill.

6. Remove the cake from the pan bottom and halve horizontally. With a pastry brush, brush away any crumbs. Brush the cut side of the bottom layer and the top of the upper layer with the syrup, and set aside for 20 minutes (to allow the syrup to seal the cake).

7. Place the bottom layer on a cardboard cake round and spread with the curd evenly about 1/4-inch thick. Top with the upper layer, and ice the top of the cake with the remaining curd. Fill the center of the cake with some of the blueberries and arrange the remaining ones around the base of the cake on the platter. Dust with confectioners' sugar and serve.

Convert It

To make this dairy, substitute butter for the margarine in the lemon curd.

9 large eggs, separated
1½ cups sugar
¼ cup lemon juice
1 cup matzo cake meal
¼ cup potato starch
Pinch of kosher salt
Grated zest of 1 lemon

Lemon Curd

½ cup sugar
Grated zest of 3 lemons
6 egg yolks
½ cup lemon juice
2 teaspoons potato starch
8 tablespoons margarine, cut into ½-inch dice

To Finish

¾ cup sugar
1 cup blueberries
Confectioners' sugar, for dusting

Chocolate Soufflé Roll with Hazelnut Filling

for one 16-inch roll

I created this marvelous roll for Passover. After its appearance elicited many "oohs" and "aahs" followed by a blissed-out silence once diners had dug in, I decided this dessert was too good for holidays only. The combination of chocolate and hazelnuts is one of those things made in heaven.

Convert It

To make this a dairy dish, use butter in place of the margarine.

Geila's Tip

You can make the filling in advance, refrigerate it, then bring it to room temperature for the right spreading consistency.

9 ounces dark chocolate (check the label to ensure it's pareve)

⅓ cup hazelnut liqueur, port or water

3 tablespoons margarine

8 large eggs, separated

Pinch kosher salt

½ cup sugar

Filling

4 large egg whites

1 cup sugar

16 tablespoons (2 sticks) margarine, softened

½ cup praline paste

1 teaspoon hazelnut extract

Confectioners' sugar, for dusting, or 2 ounces each of dark and white chocolate chips, melted, for drizzling

1. Preheat the oven to 350°F. Position an oven rack at the middle level. Grease a cookie sheet, line with parchment paper, then grease the paper.

2. Finely chop the chocolate. In a small heatproof bowl, combine the chocolate with the liqueur and butter. Place the bowl over a saucepan of hot water, without the bowl touching the water, and stir occasionally until the chocolate is melted and the mixture is smooth. One at a time, beat in the yolks.

3. Combine the salt and the egg whites and beat until they're just beginning to hold a very soft peak. Add the sugar in a slow stream, beating faster. Stir ¼ of the egg whites into the chocolate mixture, then fold the chocolate mixture into the whites.

4. Pour the batter into the prepared sheet and smooth the top with a spatula. Bake until firm to the touch, about 15 minutes. Remove from the oven and loosen the cake by working a small knife along its sides. Pulling on the paper, slide the cake onto the counter to cool, about 20 minutes.

5. Meanwhile, make the filling: Fill a saucepan with water and bring to a simmer over medium heat. Place a metal bowl from a stand mixer (or use a metal bowl with a hand-held mixer) over the saucepan, add the egg whites and sugar and whisk gently until the mixture has reached a temperature of 170°F, 6 to 8 minutes. Place the bowl on the mixer (or off the heat if using a hand mixer) and beat at high speed until a stiff, glossy meringue forms and the mixture has cooled somewhat. Fold in the butter by hand until completely incorporated. Fold in the praline paste and hazelnut extract. Chill the filling until it has stiffened slightly.

6. To finish the roll, slide a rimless cookie sheet under the layer. Cover the layer with a clean sheet of parchment or wax paper and another sheet the same size as the first. Invert the pans, remove the top (formerly the bottom) sheet and peel off the paper. Invert again and remove the top sheet and remaining paper.

7. With a metal spatula, spread the filling onto the layer. Roll the layer by picking up one long edge of the paper and easing the layer into a curve. Continue lifting the paper while rolling the cake. Roll the cake onto a platter seam-side down. Sprinkle with the confectioners' sugar and serve.

Maple Pecan Pie

serves 8

Every so often I get a pecan pie urge, which, for me, means I need to make one. On one such occasion I discovered I didn't have corn syrup, the pie's traditional sweetener. The serendipitous replacement was maple syrup, which adds its own great flavor as well as sweetness. I also used a store-bought frozen pie shell—my standard go-to when making this, especially when it's part of a big-deal holiday menu. Feel free, of course, to make your own crust, but a bought shell works beautifully here and saves tons of time. Using chopped and whole pecans adds textural interest.

Convert It

To make this dairy, use unsalted butter in place of the margarine.

One 9-inch frozen pie crust

1½ cups pecans, 1 cup coarsely chopped, the remainder whole

1 tablespoon all-purpose flour

1 cup pure maple syrup

¾ cup packed light brown sugar

¼ cup sugar

3 large eggs

3 tablespoons margarine, melted

1 teaspoon vanilla extract

1. Preheat the oven to 350ºF.

2. Cover a cookie sheet with foil and place the pie crust on it. Spread the chopped nuts over the crust and arrange the whole nuts on top. Set aside.

3. In a medium bowl combine the flour, syrup, sugars, eggs, margarine and vanilla. Stir to blend and pour over the nuts. Bake until the filling is set and slightly puffed, about 60 minutes. Transfer to a rack to cool before serving.

Allie's Apple Cake

serves 12 to 16

Allie is my mom. When I started to take cooking seriously, my mom—a great cook—passed the cooking baton on to me, which made me proud. But some dishes are still hers, like this rustic, dense-but-moist, apple-rich cake. No matter how many desserts I turn out for a holiday dinner, arriving guests invariably ask, "Did Allie make her cake?" When she has and I tell them so, they immediately say, "Can I take some home?" Need I say more?

1. Preheat the oven to 375ºF. Oil a 10-inch tube pan.

2. In a medium bowl, combine the apples, cinnamon, raisins, and ¼ cup sugar. Stir and set aside.

3. In a second medium bowl, combine the flour, baking powder, remaining 2 cups sugar, vanilla, eggs, oil and orange juice and stir to blend thoroughly. Pour ¼ of this batter into the prepared pan and layer with ⅓ of the apple mixture. Continue to layer the batter and apples ending with batter. Bake until a skewer inserted into the cake comes out clean, about 80 minutes. Check every 30 minutes to ensure the cake isn't browning too quickly. If it is, cover loosely with foil.

4. Unmold onto a rack, invert so the cake top is uppermost, and cool. Cut and serve.

One 6- or 8-ounce package of 5 Granny Smith apples, peeled, cored, and cut into ¼-inch slices

2 teaspoons cinnamon

½ cup raisins

2¼ cups sugar

3 cups all-purpose flour

3 teaspoons baking powder

2 tablespoons vanilla extract

4 large eggs

1 cup canola oil

½ cup orange juice

Macadamia Raspberry Tart

serves 10 to 12

Nothing is more delicious—or beautiful—than a raspberry tart. My pareve version tastes every bit as good as one made with milk or cream, thanks to nut milk. The tart also works beautifully for Passover, as the crust is made from crunchy, flavorful macadamias. If you want to gild the lily, you can paint the inside of the crust with melted chocolate before adding the pastry cream layer, but the tart is wonderful as is.

Convert It

To make this a dairy dish, use milk in place of the coconut milk in the filling.

Geila's Tip

You can make the pastry cream in advance and store it in the fridge. If you do, be sure to use coconut milk, which helps ensure that proper consistency is maintained. If the filling does break, make a slurry from 1 tablespoon cornstarch mixed with 2 tablespoons water. Heat the cream, stirring constantly, over medium-low heat. Stir in the slurry and keep stirring until the filling rethickens and is smooth again.

Crust

1½ cups macadamia nut flour

1 egg yolk

2 tablespoons sugar

6 tablespoons margarine, softened

Filling

3 egg yolks

1¼ cups coconut, almond, or hazelnut milk

3 tablespoons potato starch or cornstarch

⅓ cup sugar

1 teaspoon vanilla extract

¼ cup raspberry jam

2 pint boxes raspberries

Confectioners' sugar, for dusting

1. Spray a 9-inch tart pan, preferably with a removable bottom, with nonstick cooking spray. Cut a 9-inch circle from parchment paper and line the bottom of the pan with it. Spray the paper and pan sides.

2. In a food processor, combine the nut flour, yolk, sugar and margarine, and process until a dough-like mixture forms. Transfer the mixture to the pan and using a spatula or your fingers, spread evenly to cover the bottom and sides. Freeze for 1 hour.

3. Preheat the oven to 325°F. Bake the crust until very lightly brown, about 20 minutes, transfer to a rack and cool.

4. Meanwhile, make the filling: In a small saucepan, combine the egg yolks, **1** cup of the nut milk, starch, and ½ of the sugar. Set aside. In a small glass bowl, combine the remaining ¼ cup nut milk, vanilla, and the remaining of the sugar. Heat in the microwave until hot, about 1 minute. Alternatively, heat in a small saucepan over medium.

5. Drop by drop, and stirring rapidly, add the hot liquid to the starch mixture. As the mixture becomes tempered, add the hot liquid more rapidly. Transfer to a burner and heat over medium, stirring constantly. When the mixture begins to boil, after about 2 minutes, remove from the heat and stir until smooth. The mixture should have the consistency of pudding. Immediately transfer it to a medium glass bowl and cover with plastic wrap, letting the wrap touch the top of the mixture. Refrigerate.

6. In a glass dish, heat the jam in the microwave to melt it, about 30 seconds. Alternatively, melt it in a small saucepan over low heat, stirring. Brush the jam over the crust and allow it to cool to seal it. Spread the cream evenly on top. Arrange the berries in concentric circles on top, sprinkle with the confectioners' sugar, and serve.

Apricot Strudel

makes about 60 pieces

These apricot, nut, and raisin-filled bites have always been called strudel in my family, but they're actually a cross between that flaky treat and rugelach, the traditional Jewish rolled cookie, which literally means "little twists" in Yiddish. Equally perfect for dessert and nibbling, these disappear fast. You can vary the filling as you like, but if you do, be sure to keep the same ingredient ratio.

---

16 tablespoons (2 sticks) unsalted butter, or margarine, softened

One 8-ounce package cream cheese, or tofu cream cheese

2 cups flour, sifted

2 cups apricot preserves

1 cup chopped walnuts

One 15-ounce package golden raisins, or dried cranberries

1. In a medium bowl, combine the butter and cream cheese and blend thoroughly. Add the flour and stir until the mixture forms a ball. Wrap in plastic wrap and chill in the refrigerator for 3 to 4 hours or overnight.

2. Divide the dough into 4 parts. Flour a work surface and roll 1 part into a 14 x 16-inch rectangle. Spread with ½ cup of the preserves, and sprinkle with ¼ cup of the nuts and ¼ of the raisins. Roll the dough like a jellyroll, and gently flatten to create an oval shape. Repeat with the remaining three pieces of dough and the rest of the ingredients. Transfer to an ungreased baking sheet and freeze until solid, about 2 hours.

3. Preheat the oven to 350ºF. Thaw the rolls for 15 minutes and, using a serrated knife, cut them into ½-inch slices. Transfer the slices to 2 cookie sheets and bake until golden brown, about 45 minutes.

Almond Crescents

makes about 40

One day my pal Deborah presented me with these cookies to taste. Having tried many an almond crescent in my day, I put on my polite face and took a bite. But no pretense was needed—Deborah's crescents have all the rich flavor of a butter cookie and a superior crumb. In short, they're the best pareve nibble ever. This recipe is easy and works every time. I keep the dough in the freezer at all times so I can turn out a batch in minutes.

Convert It

To makes these dairy, substitute butter for the margarine.

Geila's Tip

You can make these in a regular cookie shape. Just roll the dough into balls about 1 inch in diameter, flatten them, and bake.

1. Position an oven rack in the upper third of the oven. Preheat the oven to 350ºF. Line a cookie sheet with parchment paper.

2. In a food processor, chop the nuts until finely ground. Do not over process. They should remain powdery.

3. In the bowl of a stand mixer, combine the margarine, sugar and almond extract, and beat at high speed until creamed, 2 to 3 minutes. Add the ground almonds, reduce the speed to low, and gradually add the flour, mixing until a ball is formed. Transfer the mixture to a work surface and knead lightly until the dough coheres.

4. Pinch off 1-tablespoon pieces of the dough and roll into 2-inch cigar shapes. Bend each into a crescent and transfer to the prepared cookie sheet. Bake until just beginning to color, about 15 minutes. Transfer to a rack, cool, and dust with confectioners' sugar before serving.

½ cup blanched almonds

10 tablespoons margarine

⅓ cup sugar

½ teaspoon almond extract

1½ cups sifted flour

Confectioners' sugar, for dusting

Chocolate Walnut Meringues

makes 16

These classic cookies are often the first baking test for many savory cooks, as they're easy to do as well as delicious. For just those reasons, I make them often. This version is beautifully crispy, thanks to the use of superfine sugar. For convenience, you can dry the baked meringues in the turned-off oven overnight. Just don't turn on the oven next morning, as I've done, without removing them first!

1. Preheat the oven to 225ºF. Line 2 cookie sheets with parchment paper or with aluminum foil, shiny side up.

2. In the bowl of a stand mixer fitted with the whisk attachment, combine the egg whites and salt, and beat at medium speed until soft peaks are formed, 2 to 3 minutes. Add the vanilla and when incorporated add the sugar in 8 additions, beating 1 minute between additions. When all the sugar is added, increase the speed to high and beat until the meringue is without any sugar feel when rubbed between your fingers, 3 to 5 minutes.

3. Remove the bowl from the mixer and fold in the chocolate and walnuts. Spoon 3- to 4-inch mounds of the meringue onto the prepared cookie sheets and bake until dry, reversing the sheets halfway through, front to back, and also exchanging one for the other, about 2 hours.

4. Turn the oven off and leave the meringues to dry in it completely, at least 90 minutes or overnight. Remove from the sheets and serve, or store in an airtight container for up to 2 weeks.

Geila's Tips

These are a great beginner cookie to make with kids as they are simple to create.

If you can't find superfine sugar, pulse the regular kind in a food processor for 30 seconds to reduce its crystal size.

½ cup egg whites (from about 4 large eggs), at room temperature

Pinch kosher salt

1½ teaspoons vanilla extract

1 cup superfine sugar

¾ cup dark chocolate, chopped into ¼-inch dice

½ cup chopped walnuts (optional)

Crème Brûlée

serves 4

The availability of nut milks with kosher certification has meant that crème brulée, the ultimate dairy dessert, can now be made pareve. The lush texture of this recasting suggests the inclusion of heavy cream, but coconut milk is used instead. I love the subtle coconut flavor of this version, not to mention its crackly burnt-sugar topping, and I think you will, too.

1. Transfer the coconut milk to a pint measuring cup and stir well to mix the liquid and fat. Add the vanilla bean halves or vanilla extract, and microwave until almost boiling, 1 to 2 minutes, stirring after 1 minute and every 30 seconds thereafter. Alternatively, heat in a small saucepan over medium-low heat until almost boiling. Set aside.

2. Place four 8-ounce ramekins in a small baking dish. Preheat the oven to 350ºF.

3. Fill a medium saucepan, or double boiler bottom, two-thirds full of water and bring to a simmer over medium heat. Place the sugar and eggs in a bowl or double boiler top, and whisk—over but not touching—the simmering water until the yolks begin to lighten and the mixture is no longer gritty. Remove the pods, if using, from the milk and start adding it drop by drop to the yolk mixture, stirring constantly until heated, about 2 minutes. Pour the mixture into the ramekins, transfer to the oven, and pour enough hot water into the baking dish to come halfway up the sides of the ramekins. Bake until set but still jiggly, 40 to 50 minutes. Remove the ramekins from the baking dish, allow to cool on the counter for 1 hour, then chill for at least 3 hours.

4. Sprinkle the surface of the creams with sugar, and with a kitchen blowtorch, caramelize the sugar by moving the flame circularly over the surfaces. Alternatively, preheat the broiler, transfer the sugar-topped creams to a cookie sheet and broil 1 inch from the heat source until caramelized. Watch carefully to ensure that the sugar doesn't burn. Allow the creams to cool, then chill in the refrigerator for at least 15 minutes before serving.

Convert It

For the traditional dairy brulée, substitute heavy cream for the coconut milk and bake for 10 minutes less than indicated.

One 14-ounce can full-fat coconut milk (not lite)

1 vanilla bean, split and scraped, or 1 tablespoon vanilla extract

⅓ cup sugar plus more, for the glaze

5 large egg yolks

Cranberry-Pistachio Biscotti

makes about 30

For a long time I faithfully baked mandelbrot, the traditional almond bread that's served like a cookie. Then I was given a flavorful biscotti recipe from my friend Ron, and haven't looked back. This delicious version balances the biscuit's usual sweetness with tart dried cranberries. A touch of cream sherry adds its own flavor.

Geila's Tip

You can substitute sweet white wine for the sherry.

1 cup skinless blanched almonds

½ cup potato starch

¾ cup matzo cake meal, plus extra for dusting

1 teaspoon baking powder

3 large eggs

¾ cup sugar

3 teaspoons cream sherry

⅔ cup dried cranberries

1 cup roughly chopped skinless unsalted pistachios or slivered almonds

1. Preheat the oven to 300°F. Line 2 cookie sheets with parchment paper.

2. In a mini food processor, grind the whole almonds as finely as possible. Transfer to a large bowl and add the starch, cake meal and baking powder. Stir to combine well and set aside.

3. In the bowl of a stand mixer fitted with the whisk attachment, combine 2 eggs and the yolk from the third (reserve the extra white). Whisk at medium speed until you reach a light lemony color. Gradually whisk in the sugar until fully incorporated, then whisk in the sherry, cranberries and pistachios. Reduce the speed to low, add the dry ingredients and stir until the mixture forms a firm but sticky dough.

4. Wet your hands, divide the dough into 4 portions, and working on the cookie sheets, form each into an oblong log about 14 x 2 inches, making sure the ends are equal in thickness to the rest of the log. Beat the reserved egg white and brush on the top and sides of the logs. Bake until the dough is firm, about 50 minutes. Transfer to a rack and cool, 10 to 15 minutes.

5. Place the logs on a cutting board and, with a serrated knife, slice the logs diagonally into ½-inch pieces. Line the cookie sheets with fresh parchment paper and transfer the pieces on their sides to both sheets. Bake until dry, turning the biscotti once, about 40 minutes.

6. Transfer the biscotti to racks to cool. Serve, or store in airtight tins or in resealable plastic bags in the freezer for up to 2 months.

Pignoli Cookies

makes 30

Years ago I had a date with a boy who brought me a box of pignoli cookies from Little Italy. The cookies were an instant hit (alas, he wasn't) and became a great favorite of mine. They're simple to make, pareve, and perfect for Passover. The nuts give the cookies a buttery richness even though they're non-dairy. Just what you want from a pareve cookie as addictive as these.

---

1. Preheat the oven to 325ºF. Line 2 cookie sheets with parchment paper and set aside.

2. In a food processor, combine the almond paste and sugars and process until the mixture reaches the consistency of sand. Transfer to the bowl of a standing mixer fitted with the paddle attachment, or a medium bowl, and add the egg white, vanilla and almond extracts. Beat on medium speed or by hand for 4 minutes.

3. Place the pine nuts in a small bowl. Next to it place a small bowl of water for wetting your hands. Wet your hands and form 1½- to 2-inch balls with the paste mixture, making 5 at a time. Drop them into the bowl of nuts and press down gently so the nuts adhere to the bottom of the dough. Transfer to a cookie sheet nut side up. Repeat, filling each prepared cookie sheet with about 15 balls. Bake until puffed and beginning to color, 15 to 18 minutes. Remove from the oven, and cool on the parchment paper on a countertop. When completely cool, peel the cookies off the paper and serve.

8 ounces almond paste
¼ cup confectioners' sugar
½ cup sugar
1 large egg white
1 teaspoon almond extract
1 teaspoon vanilla extract
1 cup pine nuts

Hamentaschen with Four Fillings

makes 36

These triangular Purim treats are traditionally made with a poppy seed or prune filling, but nowadays, they're available with other fillings like apricot and raspberry. My own "hamentasching" has resulted in the new and delicious fillings included here, such as dried cranberries with apricot and Nutella with coconut. Adding breadcrumbs to the fillings ensures that they stay put. These are easily made and are welcome year round.

Geila's Tips

It's much easier to work with the dough and fillings when they're cold. I like to prepare everything the night before and form and bake the hamentaschen the next day. (It's necessary to make and freeze the chocolate filling in advance.)

Crust

2½ cups flour, plus more for flouring work surface

1½ teaspoons baking powder

½ cup canola oil

¾ cup sugar

1 tablespoon vanilla extract

2 large eggs

1 tablespoon orange juice (optional)

Poppy Filling

One 2-ounce jar poppy seeds

One 12-ounce jar black currant jam

¼ cup raisins, soaked in boiling water until soft, drained

¼ cup breadcrumbs

Raspberry Filling

One 12-ounce jar raspberry jam

½ cup chopped walnuts

¼ cup breadcrumbs

Apricot Filling

One 12-ounce jar apricot jam

½ cup dried cranberries, soaked in boiling water until soft, drained

¼ cup breadcrumbs

Coconut-Chocolate-Hazelnut Filling

One 13-ounce jar Nutella, or other chocolate-hazelnut spread

1 cup flaked coconut

1. First make the crust. Sift the flour and baking powder onto parchment paper. In a bowl of a stand mixer fitted with the paddle attachment, combine the oil, sugar and vanilla, and blend at medium speed. One at a time, add the eggs, incorporating the first before adding the second, and blend. Add the orange juice, if using, and blend. Reduce the speed and add the flour mixture gradually to make a dough.

2. Divide the dough into 2 parts and flatten each to make a disc. Wrap each disc in plastic wrap, stack the discs on a plate, and refrigerate until stiff enough to work easily, at least 2 hours.

3. Meanwhile, make the filling(s). For the poppy, raspberry and/or apricot fillings, combine the ingredients in small bowls, stir to blend, and refrigerate for 1 hour. For the chocolate, combine the ingredients in a small bowl. Transfer half the filling to the center of an 18-inch piece of plastic wrap, fold the wrap over the filling to enclose it, and squeeze the mixture to create a log 1-inch in diameter. Repeat with the remaining filling and freeze the logs.

4. Preheat the oven to 350ºF. Flour a work surface well and roll 1 of the discs out on it. Using a 3-inch glass or round cookie cutter, cut out rounds. Pipe about 1 tablespoon of the poppy, raspberry, and/or apricot filling(s) in the center of each round, wet the edges with water and bring up the sides of the rounds to make a three-sided triangular shape. Pinch the dough together to seal. Alternatively, drop the filling onto the dough by heaping tablespoons. For the chocolate filling, cut the frozen logs into ½-inch discs. Fill the rounds by placing a disc in the center of each, form, and seal.

5. Transfer the hamentashen to 1 or more cookie sheets and bake, in batches if necessary, until pale gold, 12 to 14 minutes. Transfer to a rack and cool.

French Macarons

makes 24 to 30

Don't confuse these glorious, slightly chewy mouthfuls, made from a few simple ingredients, with the more common coconut macaroons most of us know. Variously flavored, and composed of two meringue cookies sandwiched around a filling like chocolate ganache or lemon curd, they're rich yet delicate—a major treat. For years I struggled with the recipe, which can be tricky, until I finally devised this foolproof method. The secret is the use of almond flour that's finely ground, and proper batter consistency. Just follow my instructions to achieve success.

If not colored by their flavoring, the meringues are usually tinted—red for a raspberry filling, for example. Directions for doing so are given, but feel free to leave the cookies "au naturel."

Geila's Tip

To make a disposable piping bag for piping all but the chocolate filling, use a resealable plastic bag from which you've cut one bottom corner.

---

1 cup almond flour

1 ¼ cups confectioners' sugar

3 large egg whites from large eggs, at room temperature (ideally, kept out overnight)

¼ cup sugar

Drops of red or other food coloring, if desired

Flavoring Variations

½ cup cocoa powder OR

2 teaspoons vanilla extract, or the seeds from 1 bean OR

2 teaspoons coffee extract or raspberry extract

Filling Variations

Chocolate Ganache (recipe opposite)

Lemon Curd (page 167)

Lime Curd (page 167; substitute fresh lime juice for the lemon juice and add a few drops of green food coloring)

Jam, such as raspberry, strawberry, or black currant

1. First make the macarons: In a food processor combine the almond flour and confectioners' sugar and process until well combined, 90 seconds. Flavoring: If making chocolate macarons, add the cocoa powder to the blended mixture and stir. If making vanilla macarons with the vanilla bean, add the seeds. Pass the mixture through a fine sieve and set aside.

2. In the bowl of a stand mixer fitted with a whisk attachment, beat the egg whites on high speed until they form soft peaks. Reduce the speed to low and slowly add the granulated sugar. Increase the speed to high and beat until stiff glossy peaks are formed, 90 seconds to 2½ minutes. If using coffee or raspberry extract, and/or food coloring, add now. Add the almond flour mixture all at once and beat until the mixture is just well combined, about 10 seconds. Do not allow the mixture to get soupy. Check by dropping 1 teaspoon on a flat surface. The mixture should spread slightly, not thin out. Surface marks should dissolve into the batter. If the mixture doesn't spread at all, give it a few more stirs, and test again.

3. Transfer the mixture to a pastry bag fitted with a ¼-inch tip. Line a cookie sheet with parchment paper. Anchor it at the corners with drops of the mixture. Pipe 1½- to 2-inch circles onto the paper. To do this easily, hold the bag at a 90-degree angle and squeeze it while keeping the tip stationary as the mixture spreads into a circle. Quickly lift the tip and form the next macaron. Let the macarons rest until their surfaces become dull and a crust forms, about 60 minutes.

4. Meanwhile, preheat the oven to 325ºF. Bake the macarons until the tops are completely dry and the macarons come off the paper easily without leaving any residue, 15 to 20 minutes. Transfer the macarons while still on the paper to a countertop. Cool and remove from the paper.

To fill the macarons, turn them flat side down and pair them by matching size. Place 1 to 1½ teaspoons of filling on the bottom half of each pair, cover with the top half, and press to form a sandwich. The filling should be visible. Repeat with the remaining macaron pairs. Refrigerate overnight and bring to room temperature before serving.

Chocolate Ganache
makes 1 cup

Convert It

To make this pareve, use MimicCreme (page 17) instead of the heavy cream.

4 ounces bittersweet or semisweet chocolate

½ cup heavy cream

1. Grind the chocolate in a food processor. Place the cream in a small glass bowl and heat in the microwave for 30 seconds on high. Stir and heat for 30 seconds more. The cream should be very hot. Alternatively, heat the cream in a small saucepan over medium heat until hot, about 3 minutes. Add the chocolate and stir until melted and the mixture is well blended. Refrigerate, stirring every 15 minutes, until cool and the consistency of frosting is reached, about 60 minutes. If the ganache becomes too solid to spread, microwave it for 5 seconds and stir, or heat it in a bowl over hot water for about 30 seconds.

chapter

II

Basics

Basics

This chapter helps you create your own great recipes. It also introduces you to bread making, a skill that provides deep satisfaction to both the baker and those who enjoy wonderful bread.

Foundation recipes are called that for a reason. Crêpes, for example, help make possible a wide range of sweet and savory dishes. They're easy to do and, once mastered, make it a snap for you to produce such treats as Sheila's Blintzes (page 159), Nutella Banana Crêpes with Praline Crunch (page 151), or your own manicotti, which you can stuff with the filling used for Eggplant Rollatini (page 123).

No kosher pantry is complete without stocks. I'm pleased to offer an exceptional recipe for vegetable stock—it's deeply flavorful and clean tasting—and one for veal or beef stock, culinary money in the bank. The effort involved in producing it is repaid a zillion-fold when you need to add deep flavor to savory dishes that would otherwise languish when made with commercial bouillons.

I'm particularly happy to present a recipe for paneer, the fresh ricotta-like Indian cheese that I serve with cauliflower masala (page 120), and that also makes a great accompaniment to curried peas.

My own non-dairy version of béchamel is as creamy and rich as the traditional kind (a recipe for which I also supply), and makes possible a wide range of creamy pareve dishes like Broccoli Soufflé (page 134) and Corn with Sage flan (page 143). Sundried Tomato and Herb Wash, a flavor-packed seasoning for cooked meats is also great as a bread dip.

I came to bread making late, but once I did, I was hooked. As good as it is in itself, Classic Challah, for which I offer a superior recipe, was a point of departure, yielding tempting variations. Peshwari Challah, which is based on the Indian flatbread called peshwari naan, is filled with pistachios, raisins, coconut and fragrant spices. It's easily done and makes a terrific accompaniment to soups and other savory dishes. Chocolate Challah began as a treat for my daughter but has become an adult favorite too. It's a wonderful snack, but also makes a mean French toast, see Crème Brûlée French Toast (page 152). You'll consider it, and the other recipes in this chapter, basic to a well-stocked cooking life.

Classic Challah

makes two 1-pound loaves

Bread making has always given me pleasure. It's odd, then, that it took me a while to make my own challah—which I did only after realizing that I'd made all the dishes for a Rosh Hashanah dinner *except* the bread. This recipe, and the peshwari and chocolate variations that follow it, are the results of my wish to change that. If you're new to bread baking, or even an old hand at it, I urge you to try this recipe. It produces a golden, moist loaf with a beautifully layered crumb. The dough braiding comes naturally once you've done it, but if you'd prefer not to tackle it, go directly to the variations whose loaves are easier to form. Actually, you shouldn't miss the variations, which take challah in wonderful new directions.

One ¼-ounce packet active dry yeast (2¼ teaspoons)

1 tablespoon plus ⅓ cup sugar

3½ to 4 cups bread flour, as needed

1½ teaspoons kosher salt

3 large eggs

½ cup canola oil

1. In a 1-cup measuring cup, combine the yeast with the 1 tablespoon sugar and 3/4 cup warm (about 105ºF) water. Stir and let sit until about 1 inch of foam has formed, about 10 minutes.

2. Meanwhile, in the bowl of a stand mixer fitted with the paddle attachment, combine the 3½ cups flour, ⅓ cup sugar, and salt, and stir on low speed. Make a well in the center of the mixture.

3. In a small bowl, combine 2 of the eggs, and the oil, mix, and pour into the well. Expand the well, then pour in the yeast mixture. Mix briefly on low speed to combine. Remove the paddle, insert the dough hook, sprinkle the mixture with ¼ cup flour, and knead on low speed for 1 minute. If the dough is still sticky, add more flour by ¼ cups to achieve a soft, unsticky dough. Continue to knead for a total of 5 minutes. Alternatively, to form the dough by hand, put the dry ingredients in a large bowl, make a well in it, fill with the egg and yeast mixtures, and, with clean hands, gradually incorporate the dry ingredients into the wet until thoroughly combined. Add ¼ cup more of flour and knead, adding more flour as necessary, until the dough is formed. Transfer the dough to a work surface, and knead for 5 minutes.

4. Oil a medium bowl with canola oil. Form a ball with the dough and place it in the bowl. Cover with plastic wrap and allow the dough to rise until doubled in bulk, 2 to 3 hours. Punch the dough down, cover, and let the dough rest for 10 minutes. Oil two 8½ x 4½-inch loaf pans.

5. To form the challah, divide half the dough into 4 equal parts. Rolling with even pressure from the middle to the ends, roll the dough into ropes of equal size. Take all four ropes and pinch them together at the top. Think of the far right strand as #1, next as #2, then #3 and the far left as #4. Move rope 1 between 2 and 3. Pick up 3 and move it where 1 was. Now reverse the count, counting the ropes from the left, 1, 2, 3 and 4. Pick up rope 1 on the left, and move it between the new 2 and 3. Pick up the new rope 3 and move it to where the left rope 1 was. Return to the right and count from the right, as above. Continue braiding by switching back and forth between left and right. Keep braiding until you get to the end. Pinch the ends together and tuck them under the braid. Tuck the top also, if needed. Repeat to braid the remaining half dough. Place the loaves in the prepared pans, cover with plastic wrap and allow to rise until tripled in bulk, about 2 hours. When the loaves have risen sufficiently the dough will not spring back when poked with a finger.

6. Preheat the oven to 350ºF. Place an empty cookie sheet on the bottom oven rack.

7. In a small bowl, mix the remaining egg with 2 tablespoons of water. Brush the tops of the loaves with the egg wash, making sure to get it into the crevices. Place the pans in the oven and immediately pour about 1 cup of hot water onto the empty sheet to create steam. Close the oven door immediately and bake until the loaves are golden and make a hollow sound when tapped, about 30 minutes. Turn out onto a rack and cool.

Peshwari Challah

makes two 1-pound loaves

This savory challah variation is based on pashwari naan—the Indian bread that's filled with nuts and raisins. To those good things I've added pistachios, coconut, spices and a touch of honey. This easily done loaf, partnered with Coconut-Ginger Squash Soup (page 61), also makes a wonderful accompaniment to Indian dishes like Cauliflower Paneer Masala (page 120). It's great as a savory snack, too.

Dough Spices

½ teaspoon ground cumin

¼ teaspoon turmeric

¼ teaspoon ground cardamom

½ teaspoon fennel seed

Filling

½ cup chopped shelled unsalted pistachios, skinless sliced almonds or raw cashews

½ cup flaked coconut

½ cup golden raisins, chopped fine

½ teaspoon cumin

½ teaspoon ground coriander

½ teaspoon kosher salt

½ teaspoon fennel seeds, crushed

3 tablespoons honey

1 large egg

1. Prepare the challah as in the Classic Challah recipe on page 188 up to Step 4, adding the dough spices to the dry ingredients.

2. Bring a kettle of water to a boil. Place the pistachios in a strainer and pour the water over them. Transfer the nuts to a dish towel and roll in the towel to remove their skins.

3. Make the filling: In a mini-food processor combine the pistachios, coconut, golden raisins, cumin, coriander, salt and fennel, and pulse until finely chopped.

4. Cover a cookie sheet with parchment paper. Halve the dough and roll into an 18 x 9-inch rectangle, making the dough thinner at the short ends. Sprinkle half of the nut mixture evenly over the dough and drizzle with the honey. Starting with the nearest long side, roll the dough jellyroll-style, apply pressure to the ends to taper them slightly. Wind the dough into a spiral, tucking the outmost end underneath the loaf. Place on the cookie sheet and cover with plastic wrap. Repeat with the remaining halves of dough and nut mixture and transfer to the cookie sheet. Let the dough rise until doubled in bulk, about 2 hours.

5. Preheat the oven to 350°F. Place an empty cookie sheet in the bottom of the oven and allow to heat.

6. In a small bowl, combine the egg with 2 tablespoons water. Brush the risen loaves with the egg wash, and place in the oven. Pour about 1 cup of hot water onto the heated cookie sheet to create steam, and immediately close the oven door. Bake until the challah is golden and sounds hollow when tapped, 25 to 35 minutes. Turn out and cool on a rack.

Chocolate Challah

makes two 1-pound loaves

Similar to babka but moister, this tempting loaf is delicious when used in the breakfast treat Crème Brûlée French Toast (page 152). It's also wonderful as is for a snack with coffee or milk. Please note that the recipe can be dairy or pareve, depending on the kind of chocolate you use, so please check labels.

1. Prepare the challah as in the Classic Challah recipe on page 188 up to Step 4.

2. Grease two 8 x 4-inch loaf pans. Combine the chocolate, cinnamon and sugar in a mini-food processor, and chop very fine.

3. Halve the dough, and roll one half into an 18 x 9-inch rectangle. Sprinkle half the chocolate mixture evenly over the dough, and starting from the nearest long end, roll the dough jellyroll-style. Bend the roll to form a U shape with the two ends nearest you. Hold the middle and twist to form a braid with four bumpy sections. Place in one of the prepared pans and, using the tip of a sharp knife, slit each section on the diagonal so the chocolate can be seen. Repeat with the remaining dough half and filling. Cover the loaves with plastic wrap and allow to rise until tripled in bulk, about 2 hours.

4. In a small bowl, combine the egg with 2 tablespoons water. Brush the risen loaves with the egg wash, and proceed to bake following the basic Classic Challah recipe.

4 ounces dark chocolate

1 teaspoon cinnamon

½ cup sugar

1 large egg

Veal or Beef Stock

makes about 1½ quarts

Your own homemade veal or beef stock will be so superior to any store-bought kind that it really pays to make and store it yourself. Note that there's no added salt in this, as the koshered meat bones will be salty, and it will be used in salted dishes. You can also enjoy the stock as a bouillon, in which case, salt it to taste.

Geila's Tip

I always double the recipe when making this, and freeze what I don't immediately use for up to 8 weeks.

6 pounds veal or beef bones, or a mixture, cut into 2- to 3-inch pieces (have the butcher do this)

1 large onion (about 12 ounces), cut into ½-inch dice

1 cup diced carrots (about 2 large)

½ cup diced celery

1 large leek, trimmed and well cleaned, white part only, cut into 1-inch lengths

4 tablespoons tomato paste

A bouquet garni made with 8 peppercorns, 1 bay leaf, 3 thyme sprigs and 3 crushed garlic cloves, wrapped in cheesecloth and tied to enclose

1. Preheat the oven to 425°F.

2. In a large roasting pan, arrange the bones in a single layer. Transfer to the oven and roast, until deep brown, about 60 minutes, turning every 20 minutes.

3. Add the onion, carrots, celery and leek to the pan, dot the bones with the tomato paste, and roast for 30 minutes more.

4. Place the bouquet garni in a large stockpot. Transfer the bones and vegetables to the pot. Pour off excess fat from the pan, add 2 cups of water, deglaze the pan, and pour over the bones. (If the pan crust is burned, skip this step.) Add enough cold water to cover the bones by 4 inches. Bring to a boil over high heat, reduce the heat and simmer gently, skimming frequently, until richly flavored, 5 to 6 hours. Add more water if the liquid level goes beneath 3 inches.

5. Line a colander with cheesecloth and strain the stock through it into a clean pot. Press down on the solids to extract all flavor. Reduce the stock over medium heat until only about 1½ quarts remain. Cool and refrigerate. Remove any congealed fat from the surface and use or freeze for up to 3 weeks.

Best Vegetable Stock

makes about 2 quarts

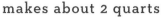

This versatile stock is richly flavorful yet clean tasting—just what you want a vegetable stock to be. In addition to its more traditional uses, I poach fish or chicken in it, or use it to thin soups.

1. In a large pot, heat the oil over medium until hot. Add the onions, celery, carrots, leek, and mushrooms, if using, and saute until soft but not brown, stirring occasionally, 10 to 15 minutes. Stir in the tomato paste and cook until beginning to caramelize, 3 to 5 minutes. Add the wine and deglaze the pan. Add the bouquet garni and 2 quarts of cold water, bring to a boil, reduce the heat and simmer until the vegetables have yielded their flavor, 30 to 40 minutes.

2. Line a large strainer with cheesecloth and strain the stock through it. Press down on the solids to extract more flavor. Use, refrigerate for up to 3 days, or freeze for up to 6 weeks.

1½ tablespoon extra-virgin olive oil

1 pound onions (about 2 medium), roughly chopped

¾ cup diced celery

¾ cup diced carrots (about 2 medium)

1 large leek, trimmed and well cleaned, white part only, cut into 1-inch lengths

8 ounces roughly chopped mushrooms (optional)

2 tablespoon tomato paste

½ cup dry white wine

A bouquet garni made with 8 peppercorns, 1 bay leaf, 2 thyme sprigs and 1 crushed garlic clove, wrapped in cheesecloth and tied to enclose

Crêpes

makes 16

Every cook should have a crêpe recipe up her or his sleeve. These traditional French pancakes are the basis of a wide range of sweet and savory recipes, like blintzes, or dishes for which they're filled with cheese or vegetables. This version is cook-friendly; make them once, and subsequent batches will be child's play.

1. In a large measuring cup, combine the flour, eggs, sugar, if using, butter and milk. Using an immersion blender, blend until smooth. Alternatively, blend in a regular blender. Refrigerate for at least 60 minutes.

2. Heat a crêpe pan or small skillet over medium heat. Spray the pan with nonstick cooking spray and wipe it out with a paper towel. Pour ¼ cup of batter into the middle of the pan, and tilt the pan from side to side to coat the bottom evenly. When the edges of the crêpe begin to brown, after 1 to 2 minutes, flip it in the pan, or use your fingers to turn it over. If necessary, first loosen the crêpe around the edge with the tip of a small knife.

3. Cook for 30 seconds on the second side, transfer the crêpe to a plate, and cover with parchment paper. Repeat with the remaining batter.

1 cup all-purpose flour

2 large eggs

2 tablespoons sugar, if making a dessert dish

2 tablespoons melted unsalted butter

1 cup milk

Paneer

makes about 1 pound

$$\textcircled{D}$$

Paneer, a staple of Indian cooking, is a fresh, unripened cheese, similar to farmer's cheese, but more compact. Cubed, it adds a welcome cool creaminess to spicy dishes, like the Cauliflower Paneer Masala on page 120). I've yet to find a kosher version, but it's really easy to make at home, and stores well in a water bath in the fridge. You might want to involve your kids in the process as it provides a great introduction to cheese making.

---

1. In a large pot, heat the milk over medium to a temperature of 180ºF. Turn off the heat and begin to stir in the lemon juice 1 tablespoon at a time. Watch carefully. Stop adding the juice as soon as the milk separates into curds and whey. Add the salt and let stand until cool enough to handle, about 30 minutes.

2. Line a colander or large strainer with cheesecloth. Strain the milk and rinse the curds under cold water to remove excess lemon juice. Twist the cheesecloth to eliminate liquid. While still in the cheesecloth, press the curds into a square, and transfer the square in the cheesecloth to a plate. Place a cutting board on it and weight it with a can to further drain and firm the paneer for at least 1 hour.

3. Meanwhile fill a bowl large enough to accommodate the paneer with water and add ice cubes. Place the paneer in the water, transfer to the refrigerator, and chill for at least 1 hour or overnight. (To store the paneer longer, drain it, and return it to the refrigerator in a fresh water bath for up to 1 week.) Remove the paneer, drain, pat dry, and cut as your recipe directs.

1 gallon milk

Juice from 2 lemons (about 6 tablespoons)

1 teaspoon kosher salt

Béchamel Two Ways
makes about 2 cups

Soy milk gives the pareve version of this traditional cream sauce, a kitchen basic, all the creamy richness of the dairy kind. Use milk plus heavy cream to make the dairy version particularly rich.

Convert It

To make this pareve, substitute margarine for the butter and unsweetened soy milk or unsweetened coconut milk for the milk or milk and cream, respectively.

4 tablespoons unsalted butter

6 tablespoons all-purpose flour

2 cups hot milk or 1¼ cups milk plus ¾ cups heavy cream

½ teaspoon salt, or more, to taste

⅛ teaspoon nutmeg (optional)

1. In a medium saucepan, melt the butter over medium heat. When the foaming subsides add the flour, mix well, and allow to bubble for 1 to 2 minutes. Whisk in the milk gradually, continuing to whisk until the mixture is smooth and has the consistency of sour cream. If a thicker béchamel is called for, continue to cook until the desired consistency.

2. Add the salt and nutmeg, if using, and stir.

Sundried Tomato and Herb Wash
makes about 1 cup

Herb washes are a "revolutionary" approach to providing big flavor quickly. Just brush this savory example over grilled meat or chicken, or spoon it over crusty bread. See page 100 for another wash recipe.

One 6-ounce jar sun-dried tomatoes in oil

¼ cup extra-virgin olive oil

4 tablespoons fresh oregano leaves

2 garlic cloves

¼ teaspoon red pepper flakes, or to taste

8 fresh basil leaves

In a food processor, combine the tomatoes, olive oil, oregano, garlic, red pepper flakes and basil, and pulse until the mixture is well chopped, but watch that it doesn't over-chop into a paste. Use immediately or refrigerate for up to 1 week.

Mayonnaise with Variations
makes 1 cup

Unlike the store-bought kind, homemade mayonnaise is richly flavored—and it's done in a snap. You can make it by hand using a whisk, with a mixer, or with a hand- or regular blender. Make sure all your ingredients and utensils are at room temperature before you begin.

1. Combine the oils in a large measuring cup.

2. In a medium nonreactive bowl, or the bowl of a stand mixer, or in a blender, combine the yolks, mustard, if using, and salt. Whip or beat until the yolks begin to get sticky, 1 to 2 minutes. Beating constantly, begin to incorporate the oils starting drop by drop and increasing the flow as the mixture stiffens. After 1 cup of the oil has been added, add the lemon juice or vinegar. Add the remaining oil as before and adjust the seasoning. Serve immediately or refrigerate for up to 5 days.

Geila's Tips

To warm the bowl in which the mayo is made, I fill it with hot water, drain the water, and dry the bowl. Then I add the yolks, which come to room temperature "automatically" in the hot bowl.

¾ cup extra-virgin olive oil

¾ cup canola oil

3 extra-large egg yolks

2 teaspoons Dijon mustard, or ½ teaspoon mustard powder (optional)

1 teaspoon kosher salt, plus more, if needed

1½ tablespoons lemon juice or white wine vinegar

Red Pepper Mayonnaise
makes about 1 cup

1. On a burner or under the broiler, roast the peppers until the skin is uniformly charred. Place the peppers in a paper bag or bowl. Close the bag or cover the bowl. Allow the peppers to steam until they become cool enough to handle. Remove the stems, skin and seeds, transfer to a blender or food processor and purée, or use a hand blender.

2. Meanwhile, transfer the mayonnaise to a medium bowl. Mix in the pepper purée and serve immediately or refrigerate for up to 5 days.

2 red bell peppers

1 cup mayonnaise

Wasabi Mayonnaise
makes about 1 cup

In a small bowl, combine the wasabi and 2 tablespoons of water. Beat in the mayonnaise. Serve immediately or refrigerate for up to 5 days.

1 tablespoon wasabi powder

1 cup mayonnaise

The Chart:
Ingredient Exchanges at a Glance

Exchanges for Kosher Foods

For Dairy Dishes	For Pareve Dishes	For Meat Dishes
Butter	Almond oil Canola oil + salt Coconut oil Grapeseed oil Hazelnut oil Margarine (preferably soy oil)	*In Order of Preference* Grapeseed oil Canola oil Olive oil Duck fat Chicken fat Margarine
Cheese Grated Parmesan	Non-dairy cheeses are not recommended Toasted ground pine nuts + breadcrumbs + salt (page 124)	Non-dairy cheeses are not recommended Toasted ground pine nuts + breadcrumbs + salt (page 124)
Cream	Coconut milk MimicCreme MimicCreme Healthy Top (page 17)	Velouté sauce (stock + roux) MimicCreme MimicCreme Healthy Top (page 17)

For Dairy Dishes	For Pareve Dishes	For Meat Dishes
Milk	Almond milk Coconut milk Hazelnut milk Rice milk Soy milk Vegetable stock (page 193)	Almond milk Coconut milk Hazelnut milk Rice milk Soy milk Vegetable stock (page 193) Chicken stock
Stocks Vegetable stock (page 193) G. Washington's Golden Seasoning Broth (page 18) Fish stock	Vegetable stock (page 193) G. Washington's Golden Seasoning Broth (page 18) Fish stock	Chicken stock Beef stock (page 192) Veal stock (page 192)

For Non-Kosher Foods

Meat and Shellfish	
Bacon	Duck Prosciutto (page 24) or duck pastrami, sliced and fried
Crab	Surimi crab (page 19)
Ground pork	Ground veal or ground turkey
Ham	Smoked dark meat turkey (page 19)
Lobster, mussels, scallops	Any firm, fatty fish, such as Chilean sea bass, or salmon
Pork chops	Veal chops
Shrimp	Konnyaku shrimp (page 19) Surimi shrimp (page 19)

For Passover

Breadcrumbs	Ground matzo Matzo meal/matzo crumbs
Cornstarch	Potato starch
Confectioners' sugar, 1 cup	Kosher for Passover confectioners' sugar 1 cup granulated sugar + 1 tablespoon potato starch, pulsed in a food processor until powdery
Corn syrup, 1 cup	$1\frac{1}{4}$ cups granulated sugar + $\frac{1}{3}$ cup water, boiled
Flour, 1 cup	For baking, $\frac{1}{2}$ cup matzo cake meal + $\frac{1}{4}$ cup potato starch

Sources

Many kosher ingredients can be found at www.amazon.com and www.zabars.com, as well as kosher ingredient sites including www.kosher.com and www.mykoshermarket.com. Look for meats at www.fischerbros.com, www.neshama.us and www.koshenexus.com. Check also vegan food sites.

For recommended brands, see The Pantry (page 17).

Canola Oil, Extra-Virgin Olive Oil, Grapeseed Oil
www.galilco.com

Cheeses

Gruyère
www.agisgoodies.com

Parmesan-Reggiano
www.zabars.com

Roquefort
www.gourmetfoodempire.com

Swiss
www.aromamarket.com

Raclette
www.kosheritalia.com

Other Cheeses
www.zabars.com
www.thepompeople.com

Chestnuts
www.galilco.com

Chicken Stock
www.imaginefoods.com

Chocolate
www.ohnuts.com
www.sharfenberger.com
www.chocosphere.com
www.mymakolet.com

Crème Fraîche
www.zabars.com

Extracts
www.allinkosher.com
www.baktoflavors.com

Food Colorings
www.allinkosher.com
www.amazon.com

G. Washingon's Golden Seasoning Broth
www.amazon.com

Konnyaku
www.sophieskitchen.net

Mascarpone
www.vermontcreamery.com

Miso and Mirin
www.mitoku.com

Muscovy Duck Breast
www.aaronsgourmet.com

Non-Dairy Cream
www.mimiccreme.com

Nut Milks
www.pacificfoods.com
www.rolandfood.com

Panko
www.kikkomanusa.com

Praline Paste
www.allinkosher.com

Ramen
www.traditionfoods.com

Rendered Chicken Fat
www.aviglatt.com

Rendered Duck Fat
www.aaronsgourmet.com

Sake
www.kosherwine.com
www.gothamwine.com

Sausage
www.neshama.us

Sea Salt
www.amazon.com

Smoked Dark Meat Turkey
www.homemadekosherfood.com
www.parkeastkosher.com

Soy Milk
www.kikkomanusa.com

Surimi
www.allinkosher.com
www.mykoshermarket.com

Toasted Sesame Oil
www.mitoku.com
www.edenfoods.com

White Truffle Oil
www.amazon.com

Wonton Wrappers
www.nasoya.com

Index

Index

Index

Index

Acknowledgments

We would like to thank Kyle Cathie and our editor, Anja Schmidt. Her even-tempered, warmly attentive professionalism has made working with her a joy. Great gratitude also to our agent, Stéphanie Abou of Foundry Media for her faith in the book and continued support. And many thanks to Antonis Achilleos for his wonderful photos.

Geila Hocherman

Foremost I would like to thank Arthur Boehm, who, after 25 years of friendship, gave his blessing, support, talent and blood, sweat and tears to help me realize this book. Arthur, you are my voice, and without your words and skill I would never have gotten this far. Writing this book has been a joy both personally and professionally. You have spoiled me for anyone else.

I would also like to thank Sheila Schlussel, Ron Miguel, Ann Avidor, Ilene Aronson, Ellen Breslow-Newhouse and Deborah Zimbler for their generosity and cooking companionship over the years. They are always available, offering recipes, culinary discourse, advice and friendship all at the same time.

The support I've received from David Strah, Barry Miguel, Naomi Stolzenberg, Ruth Rifkin, Caroline Migliore, Joan Schulik, Kim Amzallag and Susan Shay has been nothing short of extraordinary. Their unwavering faith in me and enthusiasm for the book has really carried the day. Thanks also to my core supporters and audience, Susie, Amy, Lori, Lisa (D, NY), Lisa (R, NY) and the gang at KJ, especially Rabbi Haskel and Audrey Lookstein.

I always wondered why people would joke about the need to be extra-friendly to their butcher. Now I know why! Thanks to Paul Whitman of Fischer Brothers and Leslie in Manhattan for elevating my kosher meat standards. Thanks also to my loving friend/ personal photographer Yvette Pomerantz and to my "lawyer on demand," Max Leitman. And a big thanks to Renée Green for pulling me over the pond and generously giving a new friend such great support.

Lastly, I would like to thank my family. It's rare to have such pure love and devotion as they've given me. The unending support of my parents, Moshe and Allie Hocherman, has given me the freedom to pursue this project, whether by providing professional grandparent service, chauffeuring, or listening: they have been with me every step of the way. Ditto for my brother Adam, whose flirtations with the vegan lifestyle helped me to discover new cooking possibilities. Most of all, thank you to my magnificent daughter Tess—for recipe inspiration, for your advice and opinions, which reflect your particularly sensitive palate, and most of all, for your patience. Your encouragement gave me permission to do the book in the first place. You'll never know how much that means to me.

Arthur Boehm

Thanks first to Geila Hocherman, dear friend and now co-author. Working with her and writing about her marvelous food has deepened my devotion to her, and has been a great pleasure. I thank her also for putting me in touch with my inner balabusta.

Thanks also to my friends Del Flynn, "Jinx" Gingold, John Kane and Tama Starr for caring and support. And several big licks to my cats, Chee-Chee and Poulenc.